TO TRAVEL HOPEFULLY

To Travel Hopefully

Donald Snuggs

The Pentland Press Limited
Edinburgh · Cambridge · Durham · USA

© Donald Snuggs 2001

First published in 2001 by
The Pentland Press Ltd.
1 Hutton Close
South Church
Bishop Auckland
Durham

All rights reserved.
Unauthorised duplication
contravenes existing laws.

British Library Cataloguing in Publication Data.
A catalogue record for this book is available
from the British Library.

ISBN 1 85821 884 5

Typeset by George Wishart & Associates, Whitley Bay.
Printed and bound by Antony Rowe Ltd., Chippenham.

'To travel hopefully is a better thing than to arrive, and the true success is to labour'

R.L.S.

Dedication

*To my wife Pam, with thanks
for all the love, care and support she
has given me over the years*

Acknowledgements

My thanks to my daughter-in-law Carole for her help with typing, also my good friends Pam and Dave McGleish for their support, and to my sons Graham and Richard and daughter Gillian for their encouragement at all times when writing this book.

Contents

List of Illustrations xiii
Prologue xv
Chapter 1 Square Bashing 1
Chapter 2 The Real Airforce 15
Chapter 3 Interlude 35
Chapter 4 Back to Halton 41
Chapter 5 The Far East 59
Chapter 6 Uxbridge 84
Chapter 7 Middle East 102
Chapter 8 Ely Hospital 149
Chapter 9 Further Education 178
Chapter 10 Teaching 183
Postscript 195

List of Illustrations

RAF Cardington... Where It All Started	2
Mother, Father and brothers on holiday at Clacton in 1937	3
Our wedding, July 10th, 1954, All Saints Church, Lower Standon, Henlow	22
Our first car... Halton, 1959	55
Gan in the Maldive Islands... The nearest island is called Fedhu	60
Author in ill-fitting khaki drill before a flight in the station helicopter	68
An Avro Hastings long-range transport on arrival from Singapore via Colombo	75
Young native patient with serious burns in the arms of his mother	79
Tobruk, Libya. Station sick quarters	105
Tobruk town from the top of our block of flats	115
Tobruk Garrison from the main gate	119
The children leaning on my very cheap Ford Cortina	140
My friend Sgt. Major Ali, Chief of the Traffic Police in Tobruk	147
Author getting the M. from the A.O.C. in C. at Bentley Priory H.Q	153
Aeromed Evacuation Unit, Cyprus, 1971. Author last on right.	169
Author practising with the UN at Nicosia	171
RAF Hospital, Ely in 1976	176
Teaching pupil nurses at Ely in 1977	186

Prologue

An RAF recruit in 1954 was at the bottom of the heap and there was nothing lower than that. One day during my initial training I was given the task of taking some paperwork to the Flight Commander by the NCO in charge of my flight. I knocked hesitantly on the door of the flight office where this God-like creature resided. The voice from within snarled 'Come in!', so I marched into the room and came smartly to attention in front of the Flight Commander. He was sitting behind his desk, which was covered with the obligatory grey blanket. Standing at his side was one of his drill instructors, six foot eight inches of spite, the peak of his cap down to the tip of his nose and only his nostril hair showing. Two beady eyes showed on either side of that peak. It was he that had snarled 'Come in!' The Flight Commander looked up at me in a bored way.

'Yes?' he enquired.

'I was asked to bring this paperwork to you sir,' I said. The corporal drill instructor glared at me from under his hat.

'You was not asked' he grated and, emphasizing his last point with a jabbing finger, continued: 'You was told!'

This was par for the course as I had already learned. It had been some five weeks since the three-month course had started which was designed to introduce me to National Service. This subsequently led to a career in the RAF that was to last some twenty-two years, the period of time during which most of the RAF medical branch hospital services were to be closed, transferred to the National Health Service and civilianized. In the early days one could travel the world by RAF Transport Command and wherever the aircraft put down, in many countries around the globe, the Union flag would be flying over an RAF unit. I was fortunate to have been part of this world-wide service, albeit a small part, but I made my mark and am proud of my contribution and also of the uniform I wore.

This story is also about a personal development, personal growth brought about by the many diverse experiences I had; due also to the privilege of frequently being able to help those who had little material wealth and no hope or ability to help themselves. But not everything I did or saw have I included. For this I have various reasons but the chief one is that some of my experiences are too personal. Some too are still covered by the Official Secrets Act. However I have included enough to give an overview of what happened to me and possibly to provide some idea of what a fulfilling time this period of history was. This was especially true for those of us who were privileged to serve their country in the armed forces of the Crown.

CHAPTER ONE

Square Bashing

June 2nd 1953 was the day of the new Queen's coronation. Hillary had just conquered Everest and I had become engaged to be married to my future wife; it was also my twenty-first birthday. With the congratulatory cards came a small brown envelope marked OHMS, the only fly in the ointment that day, my call-up papers for National Service. Although I had known they were coming, they were no less unwelcome for that knowledge. I had been deferred National Service for three years while I trained as an SRN at Lister Hospital in Hitchin and now I was ordered to report to RAF Cardington by 1400hrs on Monday, 4th January next. This really took the gloss off the day but with the resilience of youth, I still enjoyed myself, the bad news soon forgotten. This next seven months went all too quickly.

I woke on that January morning with a strange dread of the future. It was a cold and miserable day and I ate my breakfast and looked around at my familiar home and my mother, now a widow, full of sad looks and grief at my impending departure. I did not want that moment to pass but pass it did. Time rushed by and I had to walk a mile to the bus stop to catch the 12.30 bus to Cardington. As I was about to leave, my mother put her arms around me and didn't want to let me go. She felt she would never see me again. She was lonely and, as a widow, she did not need any further loss in her life. I must admit I had a lump in my throat and cannot remember what I said, but I had to disengage myself to start out on what was the greatest adventure of my life with an awful feeling of dread and loneliness. And this was leaving home in a world comparatively at peace. Just what people of my age must have felt when they were forced to leave in 1939, when the nation was at war, I could not imagine. At

R.A.F. Cardington... Where it all started.

least, I thought, my life would not be in danger in National Service.

I had been brought up in a rather blinkered fashion by deeply religious parents. All our home life was governed by the practices of our faith. My two brothers and I were deeply loved and we were a united family, but our beliefs dictated our whole way of life and its practices and everything that did not reflect these was deemed worldly and unacceptable. All those practices that did not reflect godliness, such as drinking, dancing, going to the theatre or cinema, the normal social activities of the time, were banned to us. Smoking, however, was acceptable for some reason. I was therefore ill prepared for the experiences I was going to have in the new and godless environment.

Because of my upbringing, I had learned to be judgmental in my attitudes about people and their behaviour and, even though I had spent three years in the National Health Service in nurse training, I still retained vestiges of these prejudices. They had been instilled in me so deeply that they stayed with me into later life. Now, fifty years on, I still feel guilty when visiting a

Mother, father and brothers on holiday at Clacton in 1937. Author holding a toy boat.

pub! But by the age of twenty-one years, although many of these beliefs and prejudices were changing, the underlying truth remained. By this time, however, fundamentalism was too simplistic for me. I had seen too much suffering and misery in three years, and this had modified my views considerably. Also my contact with other professionals had made me aware that however godless they might be, they were mainly good people with a genuine compassion for their fellow men, a factor, as I now realised, that was too often lacking in the fundamentalist movement, which was quite proscriptive and harsh in its judgements.

In 1954 all young men of my age were conscripted to serve two years' National Service in the armed forces. Some did succeed and enjoy it but many felt it was a waste of time. For those of us who were a little more sensitive than others, at this period of our lives, during which we were subjected to discipline, we would learn a lot about ourselves and enjoy the experience of free travel to all parts of the UK and indeed the world. We would encounter many interesting and strange people and places, see strange things and have experiences that would live in our minds forever.

On January 4th 1954, a very cold, dry and dull day, all this lay before me. I was also cold inside, lonely and sick at heart and despairing. What a way to start what was, unbeknown to me then, a career in the RAF! On the day in question I had taken the bus from my home near Hitchin to arrive at RAF Cardington, the reception centre for the RAF, by two o'clock or 1400 hrs., as it was to be known in the future. This journey of some 20 miles was most depressing; I knew nobody in the service and had had only a couple of uncles who had served in the army during the war. The bus journey seemed to go on for ever, yet I was most reluctant for it to come to an end. I was not a gregarious young man, being somewhat of a loner, and the knowledge that I would have to meet and share my life with a collection of strangers seemed a very unpleasant prospect indeed. In fact I was a most reluctant recruit. On presenting myself and my papers at the guard room of this cold, dark, bleak and grimy looking unit, I was given little time to think, allocated to a hut containing some thirty dilapidated beds and marched off at double quick time with the other occupants for the obligatory haircut. Knowing I would need a haircut, I had had a short back and sides the day before. This counted for nothing; the RAF barbers would have found hair on an eggshell, so I lost what little I had. Everyone shouted at you and at each other and you had to shout back to be heard above the noise. This cacophony assaulted the ears continually, so, after the first few hours in our cold hairless state, it was with relief that lights out arrived. We got into bed, two hard horsehair squabs covered with ticking a delicate shade of grey-brown, a sheet over the top and a metal frame that had seen better days probably in the First World War. Every movement set up a rattling sound; we didn't even get a quiet night.

Next day the kitting-out process started. Uniforms, ground sheets, belts, cutlery and drinking mugs, shirts, shoes, socks and so on. It came to a lot of kit. All had to be pressed, polished and 'bulled up', as the expression was, until it was to the satisfaction of the NCOs in charge of us. Some of us would be coatless and trouserless for a couple of days, however, whilst the garments were being roughly tailored to fit, and had to walk around in various stages of undress. Our civilian clothes were then taken from us, packed up, and sent home at the expense of the Air Ministry. It was as though you were shedding your skin and saying goodbye to your old life.

During this time of kitting out we had to be interviewed by the Trade Training Officer. We first filled in a form giving details of our civilian jobs, likes, dislikes, hobbies etc. On my form I gave my hobby as messing around with cars. My brother had a pre-war Austin Seven, and it took most of our spare time to keep it on the road. I had learned to drive in this vehicle, the general feeling at the time being that if you could drive an Austin Seven you could drive anything. I must admit that in all the years since, I have never found any vehicle more difficult to handle or one that was such good fun to use. The Trade Training Officer noted my interest and announced that because of my apparent expertise with cars, I had been selected for training as a motor transport fitter. Now hobbies are one thing but to spend the next two years under lorries and cars filled me with dread. I was, after all, a qualified SRN, and that qualification, I was sure, could be put to some use in the RAF. I expressed my feelings to the officer and after a lot of discussion with his clerk and himself, it was decided that, since I did not have my educational certifications and SRN certificates with me as proof, I should nip home and get them. It was also suggested to me that as I had announced that I was engaged to be married, I should consider signing on to get regular pay, which was three times that of a national serviceman. To obtain this I could sign on for three years instead of the obligatory two years with five years on the reserve, and be paid for it. I discussed these things with my fiancée that night and we both felt that this would be a good idea. Returning the next day with all the paperwork, I agreed to sign on, which was duly carried out by the attesting officer before I had time to change my mind. My fiancée's father was a retired army officer so she knew what she was letting herself in for even if I didn't.

The trade training procedure now continued apace and I was informed that I would have to go to the medical depot at Lytham St. Anne's near Blackpool. Arrangements were made for me to travel north the next day and present my credentials to the medical branch. My uniform had as yet not been tailored to fit, my buttons were still green and my boots dull and unpolished, but I was told that in the circumstances it didn't matter. I was given a travel warrant, taken to Bedford station and told to get to Blackpool as soon as possible. 'They knew I was coming. How often I've heard that remark!

The first part of my journey was to Bletchley main line station. As I descended from the two-carriage train, the RTO and his two service policemen, who were in charge of the service movements at Bletchley, collared me, viewing me with suspicion. Admittedly I looked a mess; a uniform that looked like a sack and generally scruffy. They were not impressed by my appearance but accepted that my documentation was legal and I was told to get a haircut. I think that initially they thought I was a deserter. However, in total ignorance of the ways of the service, I allowed them to put me on the next train to the north, which turned out to be a troop train full of RAF personnel off to the Egyptian Canal Zone in full kit and armed with Sten guns and rifles. I was an object of curiosity on that train, having been in the RAF really only four days; I looked the part. Men were coming down the corridor to my compartment to see the bloke who had just joined up. It was quite hilarious but most of the advice and information I was given to help me in the future, so they said, turned out to be spurious or completely untruthful. It did not make me any less apprehensive about my future in the RAF.

After a lot of stopping and starting, we arrived at Kirkham Station near Blackpool at about 2200 hours. This was as far as the train went. It was dark and raining heavily. Amid a lot of shouting and bawling, we were put into 3-ton trucks and trundled off into the night. I was hungry and tired by this time. Assuming

SQUARE BASHING

everything was under control, I just followed what everybody else did and eventually we arrived at RAF Kirkham. I joined the long line of airmen queuing up in a hangar to be processed by two corporal clerks. When I eventually arrived at the table to be processed, it caused quite a stir. I nearly ended up going to join the transport for the canal next day from Liverpool docks. Finally it was all sorted out and I left in another truck for the medical depot, arriving well after midnight, cold and hungry. I was given a bed for the night and told to report to the orderly room at 0800 hours the next morning.

The next morning I presented myself as instructed and I was most surprised to find out what a pleasant group of people they were in the orderly room. I was interviewed by the adjutant and my credentials were checked. Then I was told that I could go and return after my initial training in three months time. Well if the RAF wanted to give me train rides like that, it was okay by me. But, on my return to Cardington, it was 'We've been looking for you. Where have you been?' and so on. Eventually I came to accept that this was a normal part of service life, the left hand not apparently knowing what the right hand was doing. It was not until later in my service career that I found that there was a mad logic to everything that was done. It did work but, with half a million men in the service at that time, it took time to sort things out. There were no computers then, only telephone messages and letters.

At the end of the following week we were fully kitted out and ready for transfer to our square-bashing unit. There had been a lot of speculation as to our intended destination. Those with brothers or relatives who had preceded them into national service had reported upon the horrors of individual units, the conditions, the discipline, the drill instructors and so on. There were three main units: Hednesford, Bridgenorth and Cosford, if I remember rightly. The general consensus was that Hednesford was the worst. So when the news came through about posting, of course, to our dismay, it was to Hednesford. Now, Hednesford was in the Black Country, situated on a bleak moorland with many pine plantations and a view of the coalmines in the distance. It must have been about 600 feet above sea level and looked like the surface of the moon, with a persistently bitter north wind blowing.

We arrived by bus at midday on January 15th, got off the bus to the usual accompaniment of bawling and shouting, and looked around. Wherever you looked men were marching or being either marched or shouted at. Nobody walked; they ran or marched, so we joined this happy throng. We were herded towards a huge parade ground, which was to be literally our stamping ground for the next three months. We collected our kit, which had been thrown off the buses. There were 120 of us and we were allocated to four huts and told, 'You are now 2 Flight, No. 2 Squadron'. As all the members of our group had some form of educational qualification, we were told we were now a POM flight, which was translated as Potential Officer Material. I must admit we didn't feel like potential officers or potential anything for that matter. It felt like prison. The whole place looked like a prison camp surrounded by an 8-foot barbed wire fence with guards at the gate. However, every squadron had a Commanding Officer, each flight had a flight commander, there were some four flights to a squadron and each flight was divided up into 120 men. With some 30 men to a hut, each hut was in charge of a junior NCO corporal. Each recruit was allocated a locker and a bed space and after a lot of shouting we were marched off to a hot meal and given about an hour to settle in.

The corporal in charge of the room then instructed us how to lay out our kit in the locker and on the bed in a standard way, with every article of kit on display. The floor of the hut, which was brown lino, had to be polished, we were told, until you could see your face in it. This floor-polishing was a daily routine and if it didn't satisfy the corporal in charge, he would stamp on it with his big boots and then we would be up until midnight until it was done again to his satisfaction. The same with the kit. This was inspected daily and if it didn't meet the required standard, the bed and locker would be tipped over with the big boots of the corporal stamping all over it. Some of the younger lads were reduced to tears by this behaviour but there was little anybody could do but comply with the orders or risk the guardroom. Every day was the same. Even on Sundays there was little respite apart from the church parade on Sunday mornings.

The rest of the day was spent maintaining and polishing kit, floors and so on. The major part of the next six weeks was drill, drill until you dropped. Heavy Lee Enfield rifles were used and these had to be immaculate also. Backwards and forwards, backwards and forwards we marched on the parade ground or, when raining, in the drill hall, until we got it right. Then the punishing schedule of PT, football, press ups, every kind of torture that could be devised. If you could stand up and breathe, you went through it. If you felt sick or couldn't go on, you went to the station sick quarters and got medicine and carried on anyway. There was a constant threat by the NCO that any minor misdemeanour would result in re-flighting back and you would have to start again. This would also apply if insufficient progress was made in drill. To go through all this again was a nightmare scenario. 'I will re-flight you so far you will be presenting arms with bows and arrows!' the corporal screamed at the poor chap who failed some difficult drill movement. Also 'I'll re-flight you so far you will be junior electrician at the Last Supper'. Even this was not really enough to bring a smile to our tortured features. To drop one's rifle on parade was also a major crime. 'If you do,' we were told, 'faint and hit the ground before it does and then you can be carried off on a stretcher.'

After all this, of course, was gas drill, marksmanship, bayonet practice, survival, first aid then more drill. Firing on the range was very difficult with somebody shouting and bawling at you and it is a wonder that some lad didn't snap and shoot the instructors. Apparently Sir Winston Churchill had declared that everybody had to be a soldier and be able to fight. I didn't want to fight. All I wanted to do was to look after sick people . . . not kill them.

Being January on an open moorland, we were always cold. Water pipes froze so it was difficult to work, wash, shave, keep clean. Even the ablutions, as they were called, had to be immaculate, but somehow we managed. In the hut the only heating was a coal stove, not to be lit before 1800 hours, and this had to be extinguished by 2200 hours daily and cleaned out for each morning inspection. So it had to go out by 2100 hours to cool down then we had to sleep with all the windows open as we were told this was the easiest way to stop the spread of disease. All it did, however, was to give us all colds and a lot of bad nights and, in one or two cases, pneumonia. The cold was intense and pervasive at all times. I often woke to find snow on the blankets on my bed. Fortunately the food was reasonable – wholesome would be a better word. It all tasted the same but at least the dining room was warm. We looked forward to the meal break as much for the warmth as for the food. The NAAFI was pretty awful; tea tasted like cocoa and looked like Oxo, but again it was warm so we revelled in these few comforts. By now we were beginning to forget home and look for the little things in life that gave us pleasure. Camaraderie developed and being all in the same boat, we looked for comfort in each other's company and helped each other along.

After six weeks of this punishing schedule, the terror of being caught doing anything wrong, the calculated insults of the drill instructor, the lack of sleep, the cold, I developed a very heavy cold, went sick and was given medicine and duty. This meant that I had to attend station sick quarters three times a day to be given two aspirins and a drop of cough linctus, which didn't do any good anyway. One day an unnamed airman who had also suffered badly from cold took matters into his own hands. He has to be anonymous of course. There had been a small outbreak of rheumatic fever on the camp, which had been put down to damp blankets and lack of heating. So this young man telephoned his parents, complained to them and they complained to their MP. Questions were asked in the House, apparently by the Minister for Defence, and on the next day all the old bedding and blankets were called in and we were issued with a completely new set, which was a luxury indeed. It must have cost thousands.

SQUARE BASHING

Apparently there was a bit of a witchhunt to find the culprit but he wasn't identified and we were most grateful to the whistleblower, whoever he was. Our comfort was greatly enhanced. However, I had just one week to go before our first time off duty. A 48-hour pass home. This was to start at 1630 hours on the Friday afternoon and finish at 2359 hours the following Sunday. I struggled on, willing the time to go and knowing that if I could get home and get warm, with some of my mother's cooking, it might restore my sanity even in just a weekend.

We were all on parade on the Friday afternoon; the drill instructors kept us there until 1615, knowing that we had to get back to our huts half a mile away, change into our best uniform and rush back to the parade ground, where the buses were waiting. We bought our tickets on the Thursday evening and the buses left at 1630 on the dot. If you weren't there, you didn't get on so you didn't get home, and that was that. I don't know how I did it but I got on the bus just as it was about to leave, fell into my seat and didn't remember anything until I arrived at Bedford some two-and-a-half hours later. I then changed onto a local bus and finally arrived home at 2130 hours and promptly collapsed with a severe chest infection and a high temperature. I was put to bed under the care of the local GP until I was fit enough to travel back to Hednesford some two weeks later.

On my return to Hednesford, I was re-flighted into another flight of the same squadron. They were at the same point of training as I had been with the previous flight so I hadn't lost anything. The new chaps were welcoming and the NCOs were a lot friendlier, relatively speaking of course. I found myself, therefore, in better circumstances for the next six weeks as they were far less difficult to handle. But on looking back, I think the policy was to break you down in the first six weeks and slowly build you up again to what they wanted you to be. I know that by the time I had finished my square bashing, I was a very different young man to the one which I had been before I started.

The next six weeks went quickly. We were getting used to it and could see the light at the end of the tunnel. We were looking forward to three weeks' leave before being posted to our units. We began to find humour in small things in our situation. When we went out on sentry practice, for example, we had to extend our rifles and shout: 'Halt, who goes there?', . . . the corporal would snarl 'Friend!'. It made us fall about laughing, and when he saw the funny side, so did he, which was quite a revelation to us; he was human after all. The final task to be performed before we passed out of training was a flight drill test and the assault course. The drill test was naturally to examine the competence of the flight in performing drill functions according to the drill book and also the instructional abilities of the drill instructor. The assault course was to test our knowledge of survival under difficult circumstances. We had no idea who was in charge of the drill test, and by chance the man that was chosen was our favourite corporal drill instructor, Cpl. McNamara. Yes, a change had come over us and we did know now whom we liked and whom we could trust. Unfortunately this man was the one with the quietest voice – again, relatively speaking.

There was a strong northerly wind blowing that day and on a large open parade ground we couldn't hear the poor chap's commands. We did badly and were judged the worst performance out of the four flights. We were as crestfallen as he was and we felt sorry for him. Had it been the other instructor, Corporal Morrison, we wouldn't have cared. He was an objectionable character and we would gladly have seen him boiled in oil. His flight, of course, came top! The assault course was organised by the RAF Regiment; an obstacle course over very rough ground, with ropes, climbing frames, tunnels, water jumps, ponds and all kinds of devices to terrorize one. It was made worse by the fact that the Regiment NCOs, as we started through this course in full kit, were on the side shouting, bawling, throwing thunder flashes and shooting blanks into the ground and in our general direction. We were like a lot of sheep being herded into a sheep dip and out again. At the end of 30 minutes, as fit as we were at this time, we were totally out of breath, shaking with exhaustion and soaking wet, covered in mud from head to toe.

Naturally at such a time came Corporal Morrison, who informed us that as the next day would be our passing out parade, we would have to change into our best uniforms to be inspected for this by the Flight Commander in fifteen minutes' time. Again I still don't know until this day how we did all these things. It seemed like a miracle but for some reason, by now we almost enjoyed the sensation of doing the impossible, of proving to our tormentors that we could do what they ordered us to do. It was a strange relationship between the men and the NCOs that had developed, and after a time you felt as though you didn't want to let them down. Their attitude towards us was almost protective. If any other NCOs tried it on with us, our corporal would defend us until the end. Then, once the other NCO was out of range, he would bawl us out for allowing it to happen.

The passing out parade was held the next day and with the band playing, it was quite a experience. We were now proficient in rifle drill and it was almost enjoyed by all. How strange! We now enjoyed being bawled at! Yes, we had changed. They had made soldiers out of us in twelve weeks and we were proud of it.

It was time now for our first proper leave, fourteen days of freedom. I can still recall that wonderful feeling, marching on that Monday morning down to the local station to get the train home. It was a beautiful spring day and as we marched over the heathland, the birds were singing and so were our hearts. We had survived, much to our surprise, and really it hadn't been so bad ... or had it?

The three weeks' leave, of course, passed quickly and I had returned to Hednesford to wait for posting to a medical depot. I was moved into a holding flight which was used as a reservoir for people like me awaiting posting, and we were used as general dogsbodies on the unit to do all the unpleasant bits and pieces such as sweeping the roads and working in the cookhouses. However, I asked if I could work at the station sickquarters. I was granted this great privilege somewhat grudgingly and sent to work there as a nursing attendant.

This was my first insight into service medicine. Apart from the discipline, you had to be careful how you addressed the patients if they were of a higher rank than yourself. The standards were reasonably high. They differed little, actually, from those of the Health Service. Rapidly finding my feet, I became quite a valuable member of the team and as an SRN, I could do things that the average nursing attendant could not or had not been trained or even allowed to do.

Everybody eventually has to go sick at some time or another and one or two of our former tormentors were admitted. The most objectionable was Drill Instructor Corporal Morrison, whom I'd known from previous experience in the initial training flight. He was admitted with acute tonsillitis and had been prescribed penicillin by the Senior Medical Officer. Injections four times a day were ordered for five days and I was the one who had to puncture his rather large, fat rump. It gave me some satisfaction to see his disquiet when I advanced upon him with a loaded syringe and needle. He told me to be careful or else. 'Or else what, Corporal?' I asked him innocently. Of course there was no answer to that but the biter was duly bitten four times a day.

I was also ordered to teach simple first aid to the recruits, but I had never before had to address an audience of 200 or so at a time. I found this rather daunting, especially as there were lots of St John's first aiders in the group, as you would expect with such a large body of men from so many varied backgrounds. But it didn't matter so long as they got these lectures. I could have been speaking in Mandarin for all they cared. They were happy not to be on the cold parade ground; an hour spent in the lecture room instead, in the warm, was heaven.

After a month of this rather humdrum work, which was reasonably interesting but made few demands upon me, my posting came through and for the second time I was sent north to the Medical Depot at Lytham for disposal.

CHAPTER TWO

The Real Air Force

Now that I knew the ropes and could speak the language, the thought of the Medical Depot was far less daunting. So my second foray into the north was quite pleasant. This time I had a little more time to look around. Nobody was in any particular hurry and I recall spending one evening in Blackpool and another by the sea at Lytham St Anne's. I was surprised at the character of local people that I met; they were so friendly and genuinely interested in one, and wanted to talk. It was pleasant to go into a shop and, instead of being served by a surly, or at least disinterested, sales person, to find yourself engaged in conversation. Initially I thought they were being nosey, but I realised that they were being genuinely friendly. It was delightful indeed to meet such warmhearted people. I subsequently learnt that most northerners were like this. The Medical Depot itself reflected this attitude, as I had found before.

I was interviewed by the CO, who was a Group Captain. This representative of the Almighty even shook me by the hand and wished me well in my career. I was issued with my medical branch collar badges and promoted forthwith to junior technician. I felt very proud and as I stitched my tapes in place on my uniform, I looked forward to further promotion in the future, which I'd been told would come. It took a lot of time to achieve that rank of junior technician – at least three years – and I had arrived ahead of other recruits in three months. In fact I felt very pleased with myself. I'd also been given a glowing account of future promotion prospects in the Service.

The next day was spent in our new uniforms, complete with badges. I was posted to Princess St. Mary's Royal Air Force Hospital, Halton near Aylesbury. I then arrived at what was to me a completely unknown kind of establishment, the military hospital. Princess Mary's Royal Air Force Hospital Halton was a large red-brick edifice with about eight wards of various specialities. It contained, in its extensive grounds, a neuro-psychiatric centre, an institute of pathology and tropical medicine, plastic surgery and burns unit and several other small special centres. It was surrounded by married quarters and was next door to the famous RAF Halton Apprentice Training School. This had a huge yearly intake of thousands of youngsters who were making a career for themselves in the technical services of the RAF. One of its most famous sons was Air Commodore Whittle, the inventor of the gas turbine jet engine. It was situated in the most glorious countryside of the Chiltern Hills with many small and attractive villages and towns, and although it was only thirty miles from my home, I didn't know the area at all. It was therefore totally new to me and I hoped I'd be able to explore and enjoy what it had to offer.

The drawback was, I found, its transport links. It was very difficult to get home unless one either went by train to London Baker Street and then down to Letchworth from Kings Cross, or by bus to Aylesbury, then to Luton and then home. Very time-consuming and far too expensive for my pay. The hospital was a very busy unit. Everyone seemed to be doing their thing. As the major Service hospital in this part of the UK, with many MOD units in the area, we admitted a lot of patients from all three Services. Also quite a lot of the local gentry were admitted for treatment, which added to the variety of life. With helicopters by now developing a casualty evacuation role, these used to arrive with seriously ill patients from many parts of the UK. Great excitement was being generated when I arrived there, with a new renal unit being developed. A portable kidney unit, which was eventually to become quite famous in the early days of kidney dialysis, was also at the planning stage.

All this looked very exciting to a newly arrived recruit to the RAF, but unfortunately I was not to be involved in any of this for some years. My first duty was to report to the senior matron. I

THE REAL AIR FORCE

discovered quickly that I was only just above the bottom of the heap, even though I was a junior technician and SRN. This didn't matter; so far as the hierarchy was concerned, I was only a glorified nursing attendant. The senior matron, who was equivalent to a wing commander, told me I would do as I was told and behave myself. This to a 21 year-old qualified nurse was insulting to say the least, but I had learnt by now to hold my tongue and not get off on the wrong foot.

The Princess Mary's Royal Air Force Nursing Service officers were strong-minded women. Many of them had served during the war in all parts of the globe, often under canvas, often in difficult conditions. They nearly all came from the pre-war nurse training schools which demanded a total commitment to their patients and obedience to their superiors. They had learnt to be treated almost as servants themselves, so when they eventually achieved a position of authority, they treated their own staff in the same way and expected instant respect and obedience. Those other PMs who were younger or newly commissioned after the War were still from this background but were selected from the big teaching hospitals and looked down at those who trained at provincial hospitals such as my training school had been. There was little difference in the training that any of us had had to become SRN but the social snobbery was indeed intense even within their own ranks, let alone in their attitude to our humble position. We merited little attention.

They were, I suppose, essentially nice people but resistant to change and so the advent of the male nurse in the service appeared to many to be quite a threat to their position, which probably accounted for their attitude to such as myself. This meant that I had to work very hard to overcome the extremes of prejudice and discrimination I found. I was surprised at the number that had few qualifications in either further or higher education. I had achieved at least a school certificate at a grammar school as the result of a lot of hard work but, being brought up on a council estate, I had a lot more street credibility than most of them and so, in my youthful way, I felt superior to them. But there was no denying the fact that I was a humble airman and they were commissioned officers. We had to obey their orders or pay the price.

The nursing attendants, by contrast, being two-year national servicemen, were from a mixture of all social levels and jobs, from gas fitters to graduates, who on the whole were only interested in getting the two years over and getting out. They often looked on the nursing officers with contempt which bordered on insolence and indeed, regarded the whole time of national service as a time to do as little as they could get away with.

Some, however, were good; but most used the phrase, 'roll on demob' as a matter of course whenever they were ordered to do anything they didn't want to do. Yet others were more clever and used the time to score points from the system. An instance of this was a small tough Welshman on my first ward who ingratiated himself with the ward sisters and was coffee maker in chief to the sisters working in the department. He was a tough little chap from Tiger Bay in Cardiff, with fists like hams, but each morning at 1000 he had to lay out the little tray for the sisters, six cups and saucers, a jug of cream and sugar and so on, all nicely arranged. He knew exactly what they all wanted and how they liked their coffee. 'No-one can make coffee quite like Davis!' they cooed. However what they didn't know, and would never find out fortunately, was that when he had poured out the coffee, he would ceremoniously take out his false teeth and dip them in each cup in turn before he took it in to them. Maybe this added to the flavour of the coffee and in Taffy's case it would have been alcoholic, as he was rarely seen off duty without a pint of beer in his great bear-like paws.

There was always rebellion in the air and, on the main unit at this time, rebellion had also been sparked by a special demand. The officers' mess manager had decreed that the waiters, on the occasion of the summer ball (at which many known celebrities and local gentry would also be present) should dress up for the evening as flunkies. This really upset these chaps, who, again, were mainly national servicemen who couldn't see why the hierarchy should be allowed to insist that junior airmen be treated like this. Somebody informed the press and within a day the whole press corps descended upon Halton to investigate and write it up, to the dismay of the administration. Again questions were asked in the House and a lot of embarrassment was caused. It was slowly becoming noticeable that the average national serviceman was someone different to a wartime conscript and, of course, in wartime the penalty for this kind of behaviour would have been severe. We had a Labour government and, in the eyes of many of the men, Jack was gradually becoming as good as his master. It was enough for them to be conscripted for two years without being made to look fools as well. We in the lower echelons agreed. We felt that once again this group had scored brownie points. The skills of man management had not yet percolated through to the Services and were not to do so for some years yet. Near the end of my 22 years' service, I still occasionally came across the bully boys who felt that any appearance of reasonable behaviour was diminishing to their status. The army adage of horses first, men second and you last applied only when they themselves were under close scrutiny. Later in my Service career I usually found I could get my men to do what I wanted so long as they understood what was expected of them. In a technical service, you don't get the best out of people by bullying.

My first allocated ward was to the plastic surgery and burns unit. The War had caused many aircrew injuries, including chemical and thermal burns. I had never in my training hospital come into contact with such massive trauma before. New patients arrived each week, casualties from flying accidents in the many conflicts still going on in places in the world where we had troops stationed at the time. It is a sad fact that much expertise in both the medicine and nursing of such cases of trauma advances were made as a result of war, and this has led to reconstructive surgery as we know it today.

My role here though was only that of nursing attendant. I swept floors and cleaned things, occasionally being allowed to bed-bath a patient and make and change beds. I was kept firmly in my place and not allowed to express, or even to be asked for, an opinion. I could supervise the task of the other nursing attendants but that was all. It was extremely disheartening to have spent the four years in a very good National Health Service hospital and to have learnt to be competent in all areas of care, medical, surgical, orthopaedic and theatre work, yet to be treated as a menial. The living accommodation was a little better than they provided in initial training; the same routines and off-duty cleaning, polishing and kit inspection were in operation so we had this routine both on and off duty.

This did not really add up to what I had been encouraged to believe in Medical Depot and, after some two months, I became rather despondent. I was interviewed at this time by the unit careers officer. He told me there was a good future for me in the RAF if I worked hard. I'm afraid my reply was not diplomatic and I replied indignantly to the effect that if this was the RAF's medical branch, roll on demob. I was therefore sent back to work with a flea in my ear and I earned a black mark. After this I resolved to play them all at their own game. I would become so proficient at what I did, so particular, that I became a nuisance, showing up in the nicest possible way any difficulties in, or deficiencies of, my superiors. As the PM sisters had all trained at the best hospitals and were proud of it, as I've already said, the attitude they had amounted almost to a 'lager' mentality. Those born with silver spoons in their mouths seemed to me, as an ex-council estate lad, not to live in the real world. I found that with a lot of streetwise cunning, I could run rings round them. So I began a long uphill struggle for some kind of recognition. It must have worked because within three months I was promoted to corporal.

My fiancée and I had planned to marry in July that year and I knew that I should at some time be eligible for married quarters, but was told no application could be made until after I was married. So we had to look around for accommodation and I found some rooms that were being let by an elderly lady who was the widow of a senior RAF officer. These rooms were in Hitchin in a quiet residential street. There were only two rooms, with use of kitchen and bathroom. This was convenient for my fiancée, who was a staff nurse in the local gynaecological division of the hospital and I was beginning to find ways of getting home more easily by cadging lifts from acquaintances and became quite adept at hitchhiking. We managed to find bits and pieces of second-hand furniture and by the time of our wedding, we had a reasonably comfortable, if expensive, home to live in.

Two nights before my leave to get married, I decided that a stag night was the proper way of celebrating. I had two close colleagues by now at the hospital, both National Service men. One was a very blunt Yorkshire man, qualified as a pharmacist. The other, John, was a qualified physiotherapist, both corporals like myself. Fred's father had been the owner of a thriving transport business in the north and when this was nationalised by the government, he had been compensated heavily with cash and been made a manager of his own depot with a high salary. He bought Fred a brand new MG sports car, which was allowed on the unit as long as he didn't park it next to the CO's rather modest Austin. We all enjoyed going out in this and that evening Fred, John and myself took off to one of the local hostelries and enjoyed a somewhat scrumptious meal with quite a lot of wine. On returning late to the unit, we were all a little the worse for wear and caused a lot of noise. In fact we nearly got charged with being drunk and disorderly. We got away with it because it was my stag night and fortunately the orderly corporal that night was also a friend of ours.

We were married on July 10th that year and spent our two-week honeymoon in a caravan near a little village in Sussex. As with many events in life, the planning had been perfect but the logistics and the outcome rather fell short of expectations. Following the ceremony, we planned to leave that evening in my mother's little car but unfortunately the week before, her car had broken down on a day visit to London.

It was in a garage in Hendon and they promised to have it ready and repaired by the Saturday of the wedding. My mother would go up early to London to pick it up and arrive back about

Our wedding, July 10th 1954, All Saints Church, Lower Stondon, Henlow.

one o'clock to take myself and my elder brother, who was to be my best man, and his wife to the wedding. The church was near Henlow, twelve miles away; the service was at 1430 and we were due to arrive, in our finery, by 1400 hours. In those days we did not have a phone (few did!) and I waited at home until 1230. As Mother had not arrived by then, in desperation I went to the nearest call box and called for a taxi, which arrived at 1.30 to collect myself and brother and his wife and so I arrived just in time to be married. My mother and younger brother didn't make it unfortunately, so to their great distress and disappointment, they arrived after the ceremony had taken place, by train because the garage had made a mess of the repair and the car broke down almost as soon as it left the garage. So now we had no transport and we had to spend the first night of our married life at our own rooms in Hitchin. I had to look for a car on Monday morning. It wasn't easy in those days to find a car for hire. Service men were often discriminated against in all kinds of ways; there were difficulties with financial services like loans and housing, and all the hire firms I approached refused me or wanted a higher premium.

I eventually found a car in the next village, a small broken down Opel of dubious vintage. I was charged an exorbitant fee by a rather shadowy figure whom I never met. Instead I had to deal with his father, who declared over and over again that it was nothing to do with him, he only helped his son out and if anything went wrong it was nothing to do with him, wasn't his fault and so on. But I was desperate and I needed the transport. The car was a wreck. At first it wouldn't start, then when we did get it going and went to fill up with petrol, it wouldn't start again and then when it did, it smoked and clattered but it did move and this was all I could hope for. So we loaded up and after a very adventurous ride in which we had to cross London, we did eventually arrive that evening after having taken some ten hours to do a 90-mile journey. But we spent a very happy two weeks in the little caravan in quite delightful surroundings and gorgeous weather, such as all honeymooners should experience.

On my return, my wife went back to the hospital and our rooms and I returned to Halton, hoping to get home again as soon as possible. As soon as I reported back, I was told I was to be charged with being absent without leave as I should not have been away. As a National Serviceman, I was not entitled to two weeks' leave and should have been back a week ago. I protested that I was entitled to two weeks as I was not a National Serviceman, the confusion having arisen because I retained my original national service number when I signed on for three years. I should have been given a new number. This caused a lot of harassment and discussion with various authorities until they did at last concede that I was right but was not to let it happen again!

I now came to realise that at the bottom of the heap it was always I that was wrong. I now knew that authority always quoted the rule unless it applied to the authority itself. I was therefore the author of my own misfortune. Why had I not insisted that my National Service number be changed and so on? I was therefore stupid. That was the favourite word to describe people like myself. But one day I had had enough and I rounded on the nursing officer who dubbed me as such and pointed out that had I been that stupid, I would not have been accepted into the RAF along with everybody else and that included her. I might be inexperienced and not aware of the complexities of Service life, but stupid I was not and had proved it time and time again. From that time on things improved. I was learning how to rebel and get away with it; the learning curve however was steep indeed.

About this time I moved on to another ward in the same department, where our patients were airmen and NCOs. Although in previous wards some of the officers were reasonable men, a lot were demanding and overbearing and also treated us like menials. I had a better relationship now with our patients and I was no longer the poor relation. I spoke the same language and I felt more at home. As I had been promoted to corporal, I was allowed to participate more in the nursing care and see and understand trauma nursing at its best. Here it was of the highest standard. The two nursing officers in charge were very professional and a lot more friendly. The senior one of the two was well qualified in burns and plastic surgery and taught me an awful lot, and it was my experiences during the next two and a half years that gave me an excellent insight into burns care and reconstructive surgery.

Our patients were interesting and well informed, and for the first time I came into contact with intelligent and highly qualified technical tradesmen. I was most impressed by their knowledge and expertise in their respective roles. They were not always particularly articulate but they were certainly not fools.

To make life better for myself, I had applied for permission to live out. After a bit of a fuss this was granted. I bought a small motorcycle. It was rather tiring because of the shift duties to cycle some 60 to 70 miles a day on a not very comfortable bike. It was a cross-country journey with only one town on the route and I became very aware of the weather and the mechanical inefficiency of motorcycles in those days. Night duty, for instance, proved quite a problem. The normal shift was 8 p.m. to 8 a.m. for 21 nights without a break, and the three days' leave after this was a totally inadequate allowance to recover, but I was young and coped. It was however worth it to be home with my wife. One day while going home, I broke down right out 'in the sticks' and had to walk some 3 miles to the nearest telephone to get help. This turned out to be a small RAF radio station in the hills and I stayed the night in the police cells until I hitched a lift back to the hospital in the morning. That evening I was allowed by the police to telephone my father-in-law to ask him if he could let my wife know what had happened as it was now 10.30 p.m. He lived about seven miles away from us at Henlow and I thought he would drive into Hitchin to let her know that I was all right. By this time, of course, my wife was getting worried. My father-in-law either wouldn't or couldn't be bothered and phoned the local police and simply asked them to give her a message. Can you imagine what my wife experienced when at 12.30 in the morning a policeman was knocking at the door to give her the belated message? I was now without transport again.

The bike needed major work on it and I was without it for

three weeks or so. Some weeks before, I had lent my bike to a colleague when his had broken down and he had been unable to take his driving test. I was able to use his bike while mine was being repaired. This was all part of the camaraderie amongst the men that I was beginning to find so pleasant and useful. Very much a case of 'you scratch my back and I will scratch yours'. Later on, as I became more senior in the airforce, I realised just how much unofficial work was done in an unofficial fashion by using this method, particularly when discussed over a pint in the bar.

Night duty came around about every three months. The wear and tear on myself and on the motorcycle through living out and travelling so many miles was immense. The cost of repairing my motor cycle after it broke down was a serious matter to me. I had a travel allowance but only sufficient to enable me to make a return journey of up to 40 miles, and I was doing 66 miles. This just covered me for the price of petrol and oil at 2p a mile. I was paid out once a month. My pay was only £5 a week, so living out was quite an expense, but it was worth it to get home each day and night to see my wife, who was now some four months pregnant. Night duty of three weeks was quite a challenge; it didn't leave much time for home life. But one night when I was leaving home at 7 p.m. to go on duty, my wife announced she didn't feel very well. I assumed this was all part of her pregnancy; it being our first child, neither of us had a lot of experience in this area. However I had to leave and at about midnight the night sister in the department called me and said that I was wanted on the phone. The call was from the local hospital. The night sister there told me my wife was out of theatre after her operation and was quite comfortable. To say that I was shaken was an understatement. When I got my breath back to ask her what the problem was, I was told the matter could not be discussed on the telephone but not to worry and would I call in the morning and the consultant would see me. This was all I needed. I was given a tot of medicinal brandy to calm me down but all this did was wake me up and make my apprehension even worse. But the next morning, as I rode home and went straight to the hospital, I found my wife had had an intestinal obstruction due to adhesions from an old operation some years previously. She had been to see the GP the night I left and he took her to hospital in his own car, thinking she might have an ectopic pregnancy. The consultant saw me and reassured me. Then I saw my wife . . . oh dear she was really going through the mill now but she did recover very well. She was actually able to go back to duty after two months to wait for the birth of the baby in December of that year.

She stopped work in the November and once again our income dropped and allowances were essential so far as our living was concerned. Our first son was born just after Christmas and I now had to think more carefully about my future in the RAF. Money really was becoming a problem. The actual process of claiming the travel allowance was difficult: get a form initially from the orderly room, more questions – are you entitled to it? – filling it in. It was almost incomprehensible; then getting it countersigned first by the sister in charge of the ward then by the unit adjutant, and then submitting it to the orderly room. Eventually I would arrive at the paying counter one mile away, which didn't pay until 10 o'clock. All the usual 'Who are you? Where is your i.d. card?' and so on. If the flight sergeant decided not to open at 10 o'clock, you waited until he did, and if of course you were on night duty and wanted to get to bed, so what? One day the flight sergeant said I was being paid too much. I should not get more than the return bus fare. I couldn't argue with him or I would have been charged with insubordination. The bus fare was half the travelling allowance so now I had another hill to overcome. A submission to the adjutant had to be made and it all took time and all helped to try to break the spirit, but it would all be sorted out in time until the next occasion – of course.

All this time, of course, I was on a steep learning curve. I had now been in the RAF for another year but I felt I was getting to grips with it. Another problem with living out, however, was the lack of contact with my colleagues when I was off duty; only during the working day could you discuss your frustrations. Many of the National Servicemen were unmarried and, as long as they had the price of a pint and a bed, they were content.

There were, however, one or two perks that everyone had and the main one was the clothing allowance. Each quarter, if you had not replaced any item of clothing due to wear and tear, you were given the residue of the allowance, about £2 a quarter. This sum was greatly prized and to somebody on £5 a week (a National Serviceman was on only £2 a week) it was a considerable amount. Many of the men looked scruffy and patched their uniform and bought cheaper odds and ends from the local army surplus store, where you could get a pair of black shoes for just over £1, whereas service shoes were about £1.50. The same was true of socks and shirts; they were a lot cheaper there. My pullover was full of holes but I couldn't afford to replace it because that would cost nearly £5. However, if you kept your best uniform for parade and a surplus pair of boots were bulled up all the time, this had to do. Many a time I was on parade with my best uniform covering threadbare shirts and underwear and jumpers full of holes underneath. If it looked 'okay' on the surface, nobody bothered to look beneath that.

The same applied to kit inspections every so many weeks. You had to have one, so a set of kit was kept immaculate for this and this only; it kept you out of trouble. I was beginning to fit in with this but as I was living out, the trouble was, of course, that I had to bring all my kit in with me to be inspected. Every Tuesday afternoon we had a drill parade. This was usually taken by the station warrant officer and his right hand man, the sergeant administrative orderly. We spent an hour and a half drilling, this time of course without weapons as we were non-combatants. Marching up and down backwards and forwards, everybody shouting and bawling, left, right, until we were all hoarse. The hospital was denuded of staff at this time and I could not for the life of me see what this had to do with working in a hospital and caring for the sick. Once a month the CO held his parade in front of the hospital, when the flag was raised and everyone marched around and wasted a lot more time. The amount of energy expended on all these parades was matched only by the amount of energy that was generated by the men who devised all the different types of strategies to avoid going on them, such as going sick or being put on special duties and so on. Had all this energy not been so wasted, we could have run the whole outfit on half the staff. I was still unable to see why we wasted so much time at the hospital unit when we were always full of sick patients needing much care.

By now I was beginning to fit into the life of the ward. A reduction in the number of PM sisters was causing some problems to the RAF and so we were trusted to do more detailed work with injured patients, or at least to care for those with major burns injuries and look after men who had had a lot of reconstructive surgery following trauma. The saline bath was all the vogue in those days for severe burns, followed by skin grafting when the infection had been overcome.

This was very demanding work as the impact of disfigurement upon the man when he was resuscitated from the original injury was immense. Many a young airman, badly burnt around the face and head, was found to have no eyelids or nose or lips. And although he was grateful to be alive after the crash, when the bandages were removed, he would then ask for a mirror and could see the result of his injuries. It was at such a time that he would need every scrap of support and it took a lot of tact to help him come to terms with the disfigurement and the realisation that there would be maybe months and months of reconstruction ahead. There would be many operations and indeed no guarantee that he would be able to fly again or even look as he did before. Once or twice I saw wives leave their husbands at this time, being unable to face the future. With their dashing young pilot husbands reduced to a caricature of a man, you really could not blame the women for these feelings. Such a man would bear no resemblance to the person in the photograph on the locker. He would now have claws for hands and no real facial features.

Nevertheless it was a good time for me professionally, as I was learning a lot about wound healing and learning patience in dealing with the very slow progress made by these patients. I came to the realisation that addressing problems that were not only physical but mental, spiritual, social, and involved a host of other factors, could contribute to the healing of their bodies and minds. This was 1955 and the concept of holism and holistic care had never really been thought about or quantified, but I was actually practising it and, when later in my life holistic care became a buzz word, I realised that I already knew much if not more than most of what was being talked about. But other protocols, such as the nursing process and the patient allocation, again although not exactly quantified, had their beginnings at this time.

We were fortunate that the unit was under the control of a superb plastic surgeon, Air Commodore Morley and his assistant at that time, Wing Commander Brown, both of whom had worked with Sir Archibald McIndoe of East Grinstead fame. Both these men were approachable and were very highly thought of by the patients. However they were very senior officers who could be prickly at times – understandable in view of the fact that they themselves had to live with the demands, stresses and strains and the dismay so often shown by these poor patients when they saw the extent of their injuries. Their relationship with the staff had always been pleasant but they not only commanded respect because of their position, but deserved respect because of their commitment to the patients and on the whole they treated their nursing staff with great consideration. I recall one occasion however, when Sir Archibald visited the hospital and all our patients with special dressings had to have their wounds exposed for the great man to see. We had about sixty patients at the time and 54 had healing wounds. Each dressing took about $1/2$ to $3/4$ hour to perform. He was due to arrive with the Air Commodore at 7.30 p.m. but eventually arrived at 9.00 p.m. He had obviously enjoyed his host's company and the convivial hospitality had been considerable. The officers walked in, or rather staggered in, one end of the ward and out of the other in five minutes. That was the last we saw of them and we then spent the rest of the evening until after midnight redressing this rather tired and fractious group of patients. However, the surgeons were forgiven by the patients and we heard no more of it, but I don't think it would have gone down very well if we had done anything like this.

It was about this time that our first son was born and I had really to start thinking about the future. This way of life could not go on forever. I had another year and a half to go in the Service and what was I going to do after that? I was beginning to enjoy the work now and as by this time I was a junior NCO with my own mess, I felt I was becoming part of the set-up. A lot of my previous disquiet with Service life began to settle down as I found my niche.

Although at the time there was little chance of promotion to commissioned rank, the PMs being a separate branch, it was a possibility for the future which probably needed to be discussed at a later date as I got towards the end of my three years' stint.

Being a regular airman, I also had to attend lectures on ground defence, as it was known, which were given by the RAF Regiment. These lectures were on first aid and chemical warfare, gas warfare and so on. As a non-combatant, I didn't have to do firing on the ranges, but when asked if I would like to fire, of course I did and it was found, to the surprise of the regimental instructors, that 'You bastards in the medical branch are always far better shots than anybody else.' I could hit a bull on the target with a Bren gun or rifle with no trouble at all and I was deemed a marksman but, being a non-combatant, wasn't allowed to wear the badge. All the same it was good fun and enjoyed by all.

Another duty which affected the even tenor of our days was known as station duties, that is acting as orderly corporal or duty NCO, whichever administration chose to call them. This involved mainly being a general dogsbody after normal working hours, putting out lights in various places, such as out-of-the-way corridors and places like the mortuary, which usually worried the non-medical personnel. We also had to 'chuck out' the regulars in the NAAFI in the Corporals' Club at closing time. This was always a bit fraught as they all wanted to stay, and after they had had a few beers, it was all too easy for the situation to become quite confrontational. Still, it had to be done. After a time you learnt to cope with drunks without getting too official. Rarely did you need to charge anyone with drunken behaviour. As long as you kept your sense of humour, you would soon realize the unpleasantness involved: all the filling in of forms and the other paperwork that was needed; the finding of witnesses to back you up and the resulting generation of a lot of bad feeling. It was best avoided but other troubles were on the horizon on the domestic front.

After a few months we were asked to find new accommodation by our widowed landlady. My relationship with this lady had always been a little guarded. She was used to senior officers and I doubted whether she had ever come into contact with junior NCOs in the past. She also found it difficult to come to terms with having a young baby in the house and sharing a bathroom and kitchen, and all the extra washing and noise was too much for her. My wife seemed to get on well enough with her. My wife's father was a retired artillery major and this, I assumed, made the landlady's attitude towards us a little more accepting. But in service terms, my wife was known as the wife of Corporal Snuggs. Early in our tenancy the woman who lived opposite came to the front door one day. She was the friend of our landlady and the wife of a serving Air Commodore. She wanted to see my wife and asked her if she would like to come and clean for her. My wife assured the lady quite bluntly that she would not like it, thank you very much, and the woman left the premises in high dudgeon. The next day my wife met the lady again when she attended the hospital Out Patients department as a patient. My wife was the staff nurse in charge at the time and the lady's face was a picture when she told her to go and get undressed for an examination by the consultant. So we had to look around for more accommodation. Fortunately a padre from RAF Henlow was posted out and he asked me if I would like to take over his flat in the next road.

This flat was a self-contained unit and was the property of a rather pathetic old lady who lived on the ground floor. She had another lodger, an elderly man who originated in New Zealand and spent most of his time collecting antiques and shipping them back home. The downstairs flat was full of his rubbish, and he had a rather unfortunate proprietorial attitude towards his landlady and her house. He often interfered with us, coming upstairs without my wife's consent and being a general nuisance. After a good row with him, in which he punched me on the shoulder and I threatened him with the police and deportation back to the Antipodes, he calmed down and couldn't do enough for us. However, he often abused the poor old landlady and we were often entertained with his arguing and shouting at this poor old soul. She frequently entered the local mental hospital for treatment but we were sure that he was the cause of all her problems. She also had some alimentary problem, probably brought about by her poor diet. She could never be bothered to eat properly and suffered from continuous flatulence, so that all conversations were usually punctuated with loud noises when she broke wind.

We lasted in this flat until I was almost finished in the Service and then, in October 1956, we could stand it no more and we moved to another flat in Henlow which was up-to-date and completely self-contained. The only problem was that the woman who lived in the flat below was an ex-WRAF officer and her uncle apparently an ex-Air Vice Marshal, retired. She couldn't stand noise and felt that she was really the only one who mattered in this block of our flats. So once again the fun started, this time because my motor cycle had to be kept at the back of the flats and I had to ride by her front door to get to the road each morning. She did not approve and did everything she could to stop me using the gate by locking it. However, we overcame this and one day I went to see the newly appointed RAF nurse tutor, a warrant officer by rank.

The RAF had decided, in about 1955, to start student nurse training for a few selected candidates. The whole organisation of the nurse training under the auspices of the General Nursing

Council had to be arranged and fitted in with service conditions. The warrant officer was guardedly optimistic when I spoke to him about the future of the male nurse in the RAF. He suggested that I would do better to consider applying for a nurse tutor course as I would then in all probability be on a better promotion ladder than I was on at present and might probably gain a commission. The existing promotion prospects for me were very limited. He suggested that the first course of action however would be to sign on for twelve years, as this would give the Air Force at least some chance of recouping their investment. However, he couldn't guarantee me a place on a course; that would be entirely up to me. So after some discussion with my wife, I decided to go ahead and apply because I was now earning more than my contemporaries in civvy street in the Health Service.

My present engagement was coming to an end in the December of 1956, so in September I made an initial application to sign on. Most of my colleagues thought I was mad, as the general attitude was roll on death or de-mob, whichever came first. After a month the paperwork was returned. The wrong forms had been filled in, so I reapplied. There was another admin. upset so on December 1st I applied for the third time. The Suez Crisis had just started and I wondered whether I was going to be discharged or retained anyway. My final day in the Air Force would be the 5th December and as nothing had happened by the 4th, I made the great mistake of thinking, 'Okay if you can't be bothered, Goodbye!' And so I left to join the reserve with no job or position – impetuous youth, if you could call it that, but I should have thought more about it. Thankfully, it turned out well in the end and taught me a lesson about being too precipitate in my actions. So on the 5th December I cleared myself from Princess Mary Royal Air Force Hospital, Halton, joined the ranks of the unemployed, and started looking for a post in civvy street.

CHAPTER THREE

Interlude

The next year and a half turned into a virtual disaster. My terminal leave finished on 5th January and the pre- and post-Christmas period was spent looking for a position. The rent on our flat was some £12 a month, which in 1956 was an average week's wages and I had few reserves. My wife and I decided that I ought to sell the motorcycle and get a pushbike to reduce costs. The nearest town was Hitchin, 5 miles away, and it was here that I hoped to resume employment at Lister Hospital. So five miles to bicycle wasn't too bad a journey. We hadn't planned all that carefully, but our financial position was such that we lived from hand to mouth; at least we had no debts. On being interviewed by the Matron at Lister Hospital, I was offered a part-time night duty staff nurse post six nights a week 2 days off but 12 hours each night for the princely sum of £32 per month before tax and insurance. I had been getting, at the end of my Service time, over £45 per month plus the free uniform and other minor perks. I realised then that I could not survive on this. Cycling 10 miles a day and paying for meals on duty made it impossible and not an enjoyable prospect.

My father-in-law, who was a local postmaster at Henlow, obtained a part-time job for me at the post office leading up to Christmas. I spent a fortnight emptying letterboxes and carrying the mail back to the sorting office. I would have preferred delivering letters, but this was the province of the postmen and they were jealous of their status in the community. They felt they should have this honour because, of course, it really meant that they were the ones who collected all the tips of this season – tipping the postman was a common practice in those days. In fact he could almost double his wages during the week before Christmas.

TO TRAVEL HOPEFULLY

It was not very demanding work, cycling around the town emptying post-boxes, but at least I was earning a small amount of cash to keep body and soul together. However time was passing. It was now after Christmas and I scoured the papers, desperately looking for a job that was reasonably professional. Then the local Woolworths in Hitchin advertised the post of trainee manager. This sounded reasonable so I applied and was accepted. I was offered £9.50 a week, which worked out better than the Health Service, and a five-and-a-half-day week on days. The Manager was an ex-Army man and the Deputy ex-Royal Navy so we spoke the same language, or so I thought. I started work at 8.00 a.m. on the first Monday in January, only to discover once again that I was to be a dogsbody and that the Manager didn't like the RAF. Unfortunately he was an ex-officer, or said he was, and I had to work my legs off just to keep my head above water. Actually I think he was an ex-sergeant major. I spent my days checking stock, cleaning up, sweeping floors, humping sacks and parcels, stoking the boiler and I was expected to attend to the boiler even on a Sunday morning and bank it up so that the store was warm on the following Monday morning for no extra pay. It was very tiring work and I found it was really not my scene. Things were not helped by the fact that one afternoon when I had been in post for three weeks, I was called down to the manager's office, where an RAF Special Branch officer wanted to interview me. Everyone looked at me with suspicion.

I was interviewed by an overbearing zealot who demanded to know all about me. I countered by replying that I would tell him nothing unless he told me what it was all about. Eventually he told me he was interviewing all ex-RAF Halton Hospital corporals who had been in post on such-and-such date as the corporal club funds had been stolen by persons unknown and he wanted a statement from me. After this episode, the manager demanded to know what it was all about and, even though I told him, he was not very satisfied and told me he didn't want any thieving RAF behaviour in his store. He was a truly unpleasant man. The rest of the staff backed off and I received no support from them at all.

INTERLUDE

This was the last straw and I was determined to look elsewhere for another job.

My younger brother was working at the time for a company in Letchworth called Foster Instruments. His company made pyrometers and other heat control systems for industry. My father, before his death in 1949, had worked there for seventeen years. He had been highly thought of by the works manager and after my father's demise, the manager told my mother that if ever any of her sons ever needed a job, they should come and see him and he would help if he could. My younger brother had had bad health in his younger days and had found it difficult to work with unsympathetic employers. To go sick in 1956 was dangerous and you could soon be replaced. There were no regulations then. He had applied and been accepted by Fosters after he had been dismissed for health reasons from a firm in Letchworth, and had proved himself to be a most conscientious worker. In fact he was doing well at Fosters. He therefore asked the works manager if I would fit in and when he told the works manager that I had a school certificate, I was immediately sent for and interviewed, and accepted straight away for work in the laboratory of the company. A physicist, a Mr Massey, of the company was in charge. An ex-RAF National Serviceman, he had a BSc in engineering and we hit it off straight away. And so began a very happy and fulfilling 8 months of my life with higher pay and a 5-day week. I now had to cycle, however, 18 miles a day, but it was worth it to work in such congenial surroundings.

Each lunchtime I went to my mother's house in the town and I had my meal there. There was on-the-job training, with the possibility of a day-release course to gain a Higher National Certificate in physics and maths. Unfortunately my experience of both at grammar school had been a disaster, but I was pleased to discover that what had been rammed into me by rote learning had been retained and, with a bit of help with a lot of the calculations, it all began to make sense. I settled in quite happily and became quite proficient and useful to the company.

The job was to test thermocouples against a series of standard temperatures and to make calibrations which standardised their electrical output. It was a bit stressful to start with; you had to be absolutely accurate. Most of the thermocouples were for the aircraft and shipping industries, using gas turbines and other high-tech. equipment. The tests were not only on the finished products but also on the materials from which these 'gizmos' were made. Mr Massey was a superb teacher and also a very, very nice man. Like a lot of highly qualified people, he was rather vague at times but he was kind and supportive. Also, to my surprise, he liked pop music and couldn't stand classical music. Another one of my preconceptions shot down.

By this time my wife was pregnant again and the baby was due the following May. I was working hard and working overtime when allowed to, and sometimes, when my pay went up to £14 per week, we felt like kings. It seemed that things were moving our way and we were able to save a little. However, as always happens, nemesis struck one day in October. I was working on some calculations and I felt quite ill with a severe headache. I had to sit down. I couldn't carry on and after a rest I had to clock off and cycle home, where I collapsed with a high temperature. The GP was called and said I had flu. This was the first outbreak of Asian flu in the UK and it was extremely vicious. I was in bed for a week and hoped to get back to work the following week. However, week followed week and I got no better and after two weeks my pay stopped. Of course I had to apply for DHSS benefit, which was only £3.14 a week. This eventually arrived and by this time we were living on next to nothing.

By Christmas I was in despair. I had now been diagnosed as having glandular fever. Fortunately the family chipped in to help us by buying small bits of food. Without them we could not have survived. I was so toxic and ill, I could hardly get up. The GP came in every week and eventually sent me to the local hospital for a throat swab and blood tests. This showed I had a secondary infection that was only sensitive to a very nasty antibiotic called chloromycetin, which is never used nowadays as it is too dangerous. It was known to be so then, but when he asked me if I

INTERLUDE

was prepared to take it, I agreed; I was too ill to refuse. By now I had lost over a stone in weight and I could still only just swallow water or milk or soup. Fortunately the drug worked even though I ended up with a painful skin rash. By the end of January I was over the worst financially, though I was in trouble. The company had offered me a loan of £10 to be paid back at 50p a week when I returned. So when the GP arrived the following Wednesday, I said I wanted to go back to work but he said I wasn't strong enough. However, on pressing him, he said I could go back on the following Monday if I worked part-time and went by bus. I had no money for this of course, but agreed to do so, but how could I survive on half pay with no National Insurance benefit? He suggested that at the weekend I went out for a walk to get my limbs working properly again.

On the Saturday morning the post arrived and in it was an electricity bill for £11. This included the HP on the cooker, which was £5 a quarter. All I had left in my post office book was £11. My wife suggested that maybe I should gently walk down to the post office, cash this and pay the bill. I went out that February morning to walk that half a mile down to the village. It was a nice morning and doing something useful felt good. However, what happened next I don't know. All I remember is coming home again an hour later minus the bill and the post office savings book. I had no knowledge of where I had been or what I had done; I was still so toxic. My wife was naturally worried sick. However, I was in absolute despair, so she went up to the road to phone the electricity board and explain. They were sympathetic and promised to let us know if the bill didn't come. The post office clerk said she paid out the money but remembered nothing else about me, as she had been very busy. Fortunately I had sent the money off and I received a receipt on Tuesday, so now we had nothing left. I had to go back to work and be paid a fortnight in arrears, two weeks to go before any pay. We struggled on and the next Monday I started back, sick at heart and in body, riding 9 miles to work on a bicycle. However, as the days went by, somehow I coped, and as I got stronger by the end of March, I was getting back to normal. Even so, life could never be the same again.

I could not lift the despair I felt; how could we get straight? My wife was wonderful but she was pregnant and needed rest. One evening after the six o'clock radio news, the Minister of Defence gave a talk about the Armed Forces. They were being reorganised with a new trade structure. National Service was being phased out and a professional Armed Forces of well paid regular men was required. I said to my wife, 'That's it! I'm going back into the Airforce.' She didn't like the idea but there was little else I could do. I would apply to go back after the baby was born, I told her.

I contacted the Personnel Management Centre at Gloucester and they sent me all the details and an application form. I was offered the substantive rank of corporal and also advised that direct-entry state-registered nurses were also being given the rank of sergeant and I would be eligible for this on completion of a probationary period of six months. The terms of service were much more generous – if you were prepared to complete 12 years service, the pay and allowances were a lot higher. Also there was a reenlistment bonus of £50 – a lot of money in 1958. So what with the better pay, improved conditions and the increase in paid leave – 30 days a year plus bank holidays and an enhanced marriage allowance, my weekly pay was to be in the region of £15 to £18 initially. This was virtually double what I had been getting at Foster Instruments and I was now on a better promotion ladder in my own profession. I had sorely missed caring for the sick over the previous 18 months, but had been so concerned just with survival for us as a family that this factor had been pushed into the background. So after our second son Richard was born on May 11th, I made my application and was immediately accepted and told to report to RAF Cardington on June 13th 1958 to re-enlist in the RAF for twelve years.

CHAPTER FOUR

Back to Halton

The Royal Air Force that I had rejoined on that day in June was different to the one I left in 1956. Immediately I arrived at Cardington, it was obvious that attitudes were gentler and everybody a lot more polite. No more bawling and shouting this time. Maybe this was because we were regular airmen and not National Servicemen. They were still being taken on, but we had nothing to do with them.

Almost as soon as our credentials were checked, we were taken before the attesting officer and formally accepted into the RAF, promising under oath to obey Her Majesty the Queen, her heirs and successors and so on. Then we were told to get a haircut. That was the same! This time nobody was bothered. Kitting out, of course, applied, except we were no longer issued with all the webbing and straps we had been given before. Our uniform was better quality, better class and better tailored. We were also issued with pyjamas this time. This was living!

My disposal came through quickly, and once again, for a third time, I was sent to the Medical Depot at Lytham. They had changed the name of this so it was now RAF Freckleton – same place, different name. Once again I was interviewed by the Trade Training Officer and then by the Commanding Officer, who again shook hands with me and asked me what I would like to do. This was a surprise, so I asked him what was on offer. I could have gone on instructional duties or gone back on the wards, but he suggested I might like a job as personal assistant to the Principal Specialist in Anaesthetics to the Royal Air Force, an Air Commodore Soper. This sounded interesting. I had always enjoyed operating theatre work, so I plumped for that. I was left to my own devices for some two days until arrangements were made to travel back again to RAF Hospital Halton, which was to be my home.

Another colleague of mine, Arthur, whom I had met in my previous period of service, was also up for disposal, so we decided to go into Blackpool one evening. I was not over-keen but he was single and he wanted to see the local talent, as he put it. I agreed to come along with him and both of us, in new uniform, paraded proudly along the seafront feeling quite pleased with ourselves. Two very attractive girls coming from the opposite direction crossed over to speak to us. Arthur said hello, to which they replied 'Hey up, wack' in a broad almost unintelligible accent. This really put us off. That was the end of that beautiful friendship. Arthur just looked at me, swallowed, and we walked off.

After collecting my travel warrants and route details, I left Freckleton early on the Wednesday morning to catch the London train from Preston. I took the local bus into Preston and it deposited me some distance from the rail station. Preston was an old industrial mill town and as I alighted from the bus, I was surrounded by crowds of mill girls on their way to work from the surrounding houses, mainly back-to-backs. I walked with the crowd down the canyon-like streets between the mills to the station. I remember clearly that walk of some half a mile. The noise, the smoke, the steam of the mills, the factory hooter sounding at the beginning of work, the clip clop of the girls' wooden clogs along the cobbled streets, girls wearing brightly coloured headscarves, brightening up a foggy morning. Clogs are rarely seen today and when I last visited the area in 1996, all had gone except for a few on sale to the curious southern visitors looking at what was left of the industrial northern towns. They are now all tidied up and sanitised and you could be anywhere in the country in most towns today. It leaves a pleasant memory of those far-off days, but then I didn't have to live or work there.

The train was late but this didn't bother me as I didn't have to report to Halton until Monday. I shared a compartment into London with five airmen who had just completed their recruit training and were on their way to their first posting in the south of England. They looked at me in my corporal's uniform with a degree of apprehension. After all, the only corporals they had met had been drill instructors who had put the fear of God into them. It took quite a few minutes for them to relax and decide that I was not going to bite their heads off. It was, in fact, a pleasant journey. My wife was glad to see me, and in uniform again, and it seemed quite like old times. I spent the weekend relaxing before starting out again on my interrupted career in the Royal Air Force.

I arrived at Halton and had to report to the matron as before, but this time, although I was technically on her strength, I was to be working for the Air Commodore. She was a much nicer person than before and I was invited to sit down and have a chat. This really was different and when later that day I was introduced to the Anaesthetic Department and the Operating Room technicians, I was in a different world. I had never worked in the theatre in the Air Force, but it was very little different to the NHS apart from the personnel, who, according to their experience, were graded in ranks from junior technician to warrant officer. Medical officers were, of course, commissioned ranks.

I had met the Air Commodore in my previous service but he didn't remember me. He struck me as a most approachable man and needed somebody – me – to take a lot of the administration off his hands, to do his phoning and prepare his equipment whenever he was working, and to act as his clinical assistant during surgery. The equipment I had worked with before was little different in principle from the NHS gear, but the design of the anaesthetic machines was different. In fact most of the equipment he had designed himself. However, it was no better or worse than anything already in use in the other theatres. Even so, he jealously guarded the design patents and was very proud of them. The main problem was in the anaesthetic equipment designed to be portable. It was inherently unstable and often fell over with a crash during the operation or when it was being moved, which frightened everybody to death. Naturally I had a lot to learn as techniques were evolving continuously.

It was now 1958 and new anaesthetic agents were being developed. But these were very expensive and had to be looked after with care. They were also a lot more potent and equipment had to be re-calibrated carefully. It was during this time that the pin index fitting for anaesthetic gases was introduced. All gas cylinders up to now had had a washer, which was compressed in the yoke where the cylinder fitted into the machine. It was therefore quite possible to put oxygen cylinders onto nitrous-oxide yokes if you were busy, and there had been a number of accidents like this in which fatalities had only just been averted. The pin index was a dedicated system. On the new yoke there were a number of pins, which fitted into the lug at the head of the cylinder and so solved this safety problem. So including learning about the equipment, I also had to go with the Air Commodore to other units and hospitals and assist him whenever he sent for me.

My wife and I were not very well off. We had a good wage but it didn't cover the extras that I was sometimes called upon to purchase in this job. One day I was told to arrive at King Edward 7th Hospital for Officers in London to assist the great man. He told me to wear my civvy suit but I didn't even possess one, and I had to pay my train fare also. This admittedly was covered by expenses and I got it back eventually, but the suit was a problem and I had to buy it on hire purchase. The Air Commodore didn't really live in the real world and I remember him complaining to me one day about credit, and asking me whether I knew that there were people who actually bought clothes on the never never.

'Oh no, really?' I replied, 'How dreadful!'

He advised me one day that if I needed a new watch, to go to Gieves where he bought his. They were so helpful and let him have a Rolex for a week on approval. And then there was the never-to-be-forgotten day when he told me in confidence that if I bought my gin from the NAAFI in a crate of twelve, I would get a 10% discount. I couldn't even afford one sweet cooking sherry, let alone spirits by the caseful! But on the whole he was a reasonable man to work for and I did rather bathe in his reflected glory, which caused some degree of jealousy.

Such an irregular post, however, did have its advantages when it came to things like station duties again. I was on the duty list of the operating room technicians for anaesthetic duties and there always had to be an ORT for that, so I fitted in well with that system and that was acceptable both to the Air Commodore and myself. But quite a number of times the general administration of the hospital was upset when I was not available for general duties because I was elsewhere on my master's business. My relationship with the Operating Room technicians, after a shaky start, developed well and I didn't avoid any of the duties laid down on the ORTs. I would help with the cleaning up of the surgery and with doing other bits and pieces as required. But now, having only one person in charge of the anaesthetic room to organise it all, we had some continuity and the other anaesthetists were very satisfied with these arrangements. So when not with the great man, I made a reasonable contribution to the running of the theatre suites at Halton.

My wife and I were now looking forward to moving into married quarters at last. I had already been at the hospital for some six months and travelling regularly by motor cycle from Henlow. I had already had an accident on the motorcycle, resulting in bruising to myself and damage to the machine, which put it off the road for a month. This time there was no fairy godmother available to loan me a bike and I had to hire a scooter locally to get backwards and forwards to Halton from Henlow – more expense, of course, but it had to be done. I was getting the allowances and so had to travel. It was pretty frustrating travelling by a 100cc scooter after a 500cc AJS motorcycle.

One morning, out in the sticks at about 7.15 a.m. on a reasonably sunny morning, the machine gave up the ghost. In those days the 2-stroke engines were far less efficient than the 4-stroke motorcycle, which isn't saying a lot. The plug fouled up and I stopped to clean it. I noticed some distance ahead, about a quarter of a mile, a green Ford Eight stopped on the side of the road and a teenage girl looking over her shoulder towards me. She was wheeling a bicycle and looking harassed. I had by now got my scooter started and as I moved off, she started running towards me down the road. At that moment a young man came running out of the field on the left of the road, jumped over a gate in one bound, dashed to the green Ford Eight and drove off at speed – if a Ford Eight could be said to speed. I managed to get a look at the car and noted its number. Then I stopped by the girl, who was by now looking quite flustered.

'What's the matter?' I asked.

She replied that that chap had attracted her notice when she was on her way to work and he was doing funny things in the field. I assumed he was doing something dirty or illegal as he was doing his trousers up as he ran to the car. But she was flustered and I reassured her and rather foolishly gave her my telephone number at the hospital. I drove on once she had assured me that she would be all right. I reported the matter to the Guard Room as soon as I got to the hospital and later I was advised by the guard commander to repeat the whole episode to the civil police. This I did and waited while the local bobby took it all down in longhand blow by blow from my description of the incident. Some days later I was issued with a summons to appear in court as a witness at Linslade near Leighton Buzzard, and with the permission of the hospital adjutant, duly presented myself.

It happened to be a morning of indecency cases and I spent an entertaining morning listening to a chapter of excuses from the assembled malefactors who had been caught. When I was eventually called into the witness box, I said my piece and replied to the questions by the prosecuting officer. After this I sat in the body of the court with one of the police officers, who commented on the various cases sotto voce. It was amusing, to say the least, to hear what he had to say and I found it hard not to laugh at some of the hard-luck stories that we listened to and also the terms that were used, particularly by the female victims of the incidents. They had to be schooled by the police to phrase their answers in a genteel fashion so as not to offend sensibilities. To hear a lady who had had some yobbo wearing a dirty raincoat expose himself to her, repeat that he was holding and exposing his person, was, to put it mildly, ludicrous in the extreme to me as a youngster. Quite unused to the criminal fraternity, I listened carefully to the accused in my case as the magistrate questioned the offender as to what he was doing in the field. The rather inadequate looking chap replied that as he had an old war wound – remember, the chap couldn't have been more than 25 and this was 1958, 13 years after the cessation of hostilities – he couldn't control himself and had been taken short and had to relieve himself there and then. The magistrate pointed out that when the constable went to the field with the chap afterwards to look for evidence, there was none. The chap said heavily that this was because he was a very tidy man and he didn't like leaving things like that around, so he had wrapped it up in newspaper, taken it to work and flushed it down the toilet. At this the policeman sitting next to me said under his breath,

'I'm not surprised the beak's annoyed. It's his field, he's the local farmer.'

This rather pathetic figure was fined £5 for an indecent act rather than indecent exposure. After the case was over, the clerk of the court collected me and asked me how much I wanted. I replied I didn't want anything, only a gallon of fuel and he said,

'Oh come on! Have a meal out of him – after all he's the one who's got to pay.' So I collected £5 in cash, his costs and had a drink on him. This was, of course, only one of the many incidents that occurred on the road while I was travelling.

You were not so well insulated from the world on a motorcycle as you would have been in a car so it was a relief when in January 1958 I hung up my crash helmet for good and we moved into married quarters for the first time. Married quarters in those days had a life of their own. We formed quite a community surrounding the hospital and main camp and it was nice to make friends and to see a larger selection of RAF tradesmen in their normal environment. The quarters were reasonably priced, about one fifth of one's weekly wage; they were adequate, with the necessities of life, and were heated with coal fires. The coal was delivered monthly and cost about 35p a hundredweight. A hundredweight of coal didn't go far but it was wonderful to get home after a busy day in the operating theatre and sit down by a nice coal fire. My wife settled in very well with the two boys, who had their own bedroom, and although we had only one room downstairs apart from a small scullery with a bathroom off, we were quite comfortable. Married quarters had sheets provided weekly but many wives would not use these and preferred their own bedding. The standard of cleanliness had to be checked and, to the annoyance of most wives, was inspected by the Families' Officer once a year. The organisation did not require a lot but there seemed to be a competitive spirit amongst the wives to have the most highly polished married quarters they could achieve.

There was, however, no whining or complaining. The tenancy agreement was quite specific. If you didn't fulfil your part, you lost your right to airman's married quarters. The allocation of quarters depended upon the length of time in the Service, the number, age and sex of children and the number, if any, of unaccompanied postings the head of the house had had in the previous five years, which earned him double points. On the whole the quarters were comfortable and adequate and maintained to a reasonable standard and condition, but all the furniture was the same: identical colours and everything standardized. However we all tried to add a little bit of individuality with nick-nacks and pictures. We were not allowed to paint the walls. If anyone did, on marching out as it was called, the paint would have to be removed and returned to RAF colours at the individual's own expense. Otherwise the RAF would repaint it and charge him for it.

Accidents occasionally happened and the Families Officer was usually quite helpful. I remember one Sunday morning at 8.00 a.m. I broke the toilet pan. My wife was some eight months pregnant again and needed it every hour, so it was quite a disaster. I had injured my hand mending someone's car and had had the hand put in plaster. I had also been put on antibiotics, which upset my gut, and after an urgent call of nature on a Sunday morning, I put my hand above the toilet for a little bottle of Brobat with which to flush the loo. Unfortunately I had forgotten the plaster and couldn't grip the heavy glass bottle properly. It slipped through my grasp and went straight down with unerring aim through the bottom of the pan with a dreadful crash. I was, to say the least, stunned. My wife was, of course, most annoyed but I contacted the guardroom straight away and within an hour the plumber arrived and fitted a new pan. This was Sunday morning. My wife's face was a picture when she asked the plumber, on completing his work, how soon she could use the toilet and he replied,

'Well about a fortnight, Madam,' and then hastily corrected his statement when he saw the result of absolute horror on her face. 'No,' he said, 'You can use it straight away.'

There were quite a lot of characters on the unit in quarters. My next-door neighbour was a car fanatic. John owned an old Opel car but wanted a Jaguar. He was a corporal airframe fitter and this was quite an ambition. He had rather a timid wife and a lovely little daughter of some two summers, who frequently wandered around the patch with her face covered in chocolate. Sadly these two seemed to be second in his order of priorities. However, John's obsession with the Jaguar continued even though he could not possibly have afforded to run a big car, let alone buy one. But one day he saw an advertisement in the paper offering a Jaguar Mark 7 for sale for £250. This was the price in 1960 and he decided to trade in his Opel in part exchange and finance the rest on HP. He admitted to me that he couldn't afford it and tried all ways to raise the cash, so when one of his colleagues offered him £250 for his own car, he took the plunge and sold it to him for cash. The next day he arranged to go to London to get the Jaguar. John was also a betting man and there was a big race the following day, and he now spent hours of indecision before he took the afternoon train to London, agonising whether he should put all that £250 down on a horse which was priced at 5 to 1. In the event, caution triumphed and he let the race go by and promptly regretted it when the horse came in at 20 to 1. Poor John! He could have got two new Jags for that but he did get the Mark 7, which stood outside his quarter for the next year. He couldn't afford to run it – anyway only to the petrol pump and back.

Another great character lived almost opposite us. Arthur was a welder and a sergeant instructor at the apprentice school. He was a great hunting, shooting and fishing man and he and his wife Beth had a little daughter who sadly had hydrocephalus. But Beth had a host of friends and neighbours. Many of these people were very well-connected, of a middle class background. Arthur and his brother, who was an RAF apprentice, were very good at fixing things both materially and socially. He was good company and a very likeable rogue. He had a big American car and spent much time buying and selling cars and doing up motorcycles. He was a great help to me and gave me a lot of tips on re-spraying my car and helping me to keep it on the road.

Most of his actions were slightly illegal; buying and selling property in the Royal Air Force was not allowed. However, one day he bought an old Ariel Square Four motorcycle, a most powerful machine with a 4 cylinder air-cooled 1000cc engine and a kick like a mule. He took this thing to bits, rebuilt it and fitted a sidecar chassis to act as a stabiliser, often chatting to me as he was working on it.

One day after it was completed, he walked over to my quarter and asked me if he could borrow my foot pump as he had a soft tyre. I went with him to my garage to fetch it and outside his garage were a number of air apprentices gathered around his Square Four. Now, apprentices were not allowed any type of vehicle at all, even if they had a driving licence. Most of them were under seventeen anyway but Arthur was in the process of selling this guided missile to three of them, all colonial servicemen of the Malaysian Air Force.

In those days it was only the real aristocracy in the colonies who could get into the RAF apprentice branch and these three were all wearing blue turbans and very smart uniforms. I asked them what they were doing and they replied that they were

BACK TO HALTON

buying the bike from the Sergeant to go touring on the continent. When asked if any of them could ride a motorcycle, they all denied that they could but said that Arthur would give them some instruction. And when were they going? I asked. 'Tomorrow,' they replied. Arthur was not in the least abashed by their revelation and when I expressed my disquiet, he didn't want to know. None of them had a licence to drive either. However, Arthur, after pumping up the tyres, gave them some instruction and I walked away shaking my head and went back home. I was sitting in my house and I happened to look out onto the road where I saw him talking to these lads, showing them how the thing worked. Suddenly there was a roar from the engine. I looked up just in time to see these three turbaned apprentices hurtling up the road, one driving, one on the pillion and the other clutching the sidecar frame, which was just a plank. I saw them driving at full speed, totally out of control, straight into the front of a brand new Ford Consul which was owned by Arthur's neighbour. There was a sickening crash and silence. I rushed out of my house to help but fortunately all three, though shaken, were not injured. The bike was a total 'write-off' and the front of the Consul was very, very battered. Its owner was furious. Arthur just stood surveying the scene with his hands in his pockets, 'Oh you bad buggers!' he said, and with that he walked indoors.

By now the RAF medical branch was getting active in student nurse training and a number of ex-medical secretarial NCOs and also WRAF personnel were on courses at the hospital. By and large, the men were experienced airmen and had learnt their basic nursing skills on the job. So all had to be gently guided into the ways of righteousness by the tutors and those qualified nurses who liked teaching. I was one of these and made friends with some, who were sent to the operating theatre for training in theatre skills. They were mainly senior NCOs who had to be treated with kid gloves as befitted their status. I had just been promoted to sergeant but many of these were flight sergeants or warrant officers. They still had to be treated carefully even though they were students.

Their training was according to the rules of the General Nursing Council and every year its inspectors would visit the hospital and talk to individual students about their training. This generated some little annoyance, having civilians inspecting a Service hospital, but they were the ones who had the whip hand and if training was not carried out according to the demands of the syllabus, the certificate for training could be revoked.

The GNC inspection each year was rivalled only by the other two great inspections of the year, the pre-Air Officer Commanding and the Air Officer Commanding inspections, both of which meant that the whole unit was scrubbed from top to bottom. A series of parades was initiated. The last major one, when the AOC himself inspected us all in a parade and a subsequent march past with him at the saluting base, was held with the apprentices' band present. All in all a grand affair and in its way quite enjoyable. I could never really disagree with these inspections; they did make you think and clean the place out of all the surplus rubbish, but it did involve an awful lot of people and a huge amount of work.

Other inspections, however, were minor in comparison, such as the matron-in-chief or the principal medical officer visits. These were mainly technical visits looking at the quality of work and standards maintained not only in nursing but also in administration of the unit. Morale was always the main consideration and this was often reflected in the sick return which was made by the CO each month. If the sickness level went up, it was the CO and his administration that was queried, not the competence of the SMO and his staff. Low morale – high sickness rate.

Each RAF hospital was fully staffed in most major specialities for the patients but a very efficient personnel medical service was on offer for the staff of all ranks. This was run in the same way as the GP's clinic but with referrals, if necessary, to the consultants of the hospital. You couldn't just ask the consultant to look at you and even if you were sick, you had to go through the correct channels to get medicine and care and had to attend the medical inspection room, the MI Room, as it was known.

BACK TO HALTON

After going sick, there were the usual categories: medicine and duty, light duties, off duties for specified periods of time, admission to hospital and so on. A form was given to you when the appropriate therapy or treatment was prescribed, and for the RAF it was form 624 with the category written on it. You could only be sick or off-duty for so long and then you were downgraded by a proper medical board. It was usually the Wing Commander Registrar who decided what was to happen to you. If you were downgraded medically, quite often it meant that you were therefore not eligible for promotion or eligible for posting either at home or abroad. Alternatively, a decision was made regarding your future in the RAF itself. It was possible to pull the wool over the MO's eyes occasionally, as I will describe later, but on the whole the RAF medical officers had seen it all before. The system was organized so that any malingerer did not get away with it for long. In a well-run unit the rate of malingering was low. In a population of, shall we say, 500 men, you were guaranteed to have, as in any population, a proportion of men who enjoyed ill health and made the most of it.

One of the main roles of medical service was to maintain and monitor health with frequent medical examinations and to give all the usual inoculations needed for world-wide travel. A number of personnel on each unit always had to be up to date with their inoculations in case they were called upon for overseas service quickly. I had been called out a number of times at midnight and had found myself next morning on some foreign shore, so it was essential to be prepared. All other parts of the service which administered us and maintained our state of readiness were dealt with down the road by departments of the main unit, such as Accounts and Clothing Stores. All in all, the RAF was a microcosm of life within a macrocosm; on the whole a very efficient organisation with answers to most problems.

My work continued in the operating theatre and got more interesting as we went along. The staff came and went. Most of the doctors and trained nursing staff were from the bigger training and medical schools at the time, so the amount of experience brought into the Service was quite exceptional. I remember, when my career in the Royal Air Force finally ended and I returned to the Health Service, how very parochial everything was: 'We don't do it like that here!'

The Service was indeed quite innovative and not averse to looking at new ideas and new practices from other hospitals. I visited quite a number of RAF hospitals and other units with the Air Commodore. These visits were often liaison visits and I saw parts of the Royal Air Force that a lot of people in less interesting jobs never saw. The School of Aviation Medicine at Farnborough was a most interesting place to visit and to see the Air Commodore talk to the technicians looking at the medical problems of flying fast jet aircraft was fascinating. But I always had to remember, or be sharply reminded of the fact, that I was not an officer and to keep my mouth shut unless I was spoken to.

One day after visiting Farnborough, we went to see a factory where a lot of the high-tech anaesthetic equipment was made. The RAF used a lot of these machines and, after we had been shown around the factory, the Air Commodore asked the managing director if he would show me round his pet project. Round the back of his factory he was building a kit car with a V12 Jaguar engine. It had been beautifully put together but he was having trouble with road testing. It suffered from fuel starvation. I noted that the fuel pump in the engine compartment was bolted to the bulkhead at the level of the carburettor and I observed to this very technical man that surely this pump should be at the bottom of the engine, to be filled by gravity from the tank and then pumped to the engine, so that it wasn't sucking and blowing. The unit was not designed for this. He looked at me blankly through his thick glasses for a moment and then smiled. 'Of course!' he said, 'I didn't think of that.' My standing with the Air Commodore went right up at that point and we left the place in very high spirits.

So life settled down into a comfortable existence in our small quarter and, with a new baby on the way, I applied for a larger house. On the birth of our daughter Gillian, we were allocated a three-bedroom warrant officers' quarter about 200 yards away from our original home. This was very much nicer to live in, with a separate sitting room and a dining room. The only problem was that it had an Aga-type cooker in the kitchen, which heated the water and ran on smokeless fuel. This took a lot of cleaning and a lot of practice and I used a tonne of fuel within a matter of 2 weeks until I got the hang of it. It wasn't quite so disastrous financially, as by now I was a sergeant on far better pay. I had also decided to make the RAF my main career and bitten the bullet to sign on to complete service to my 55th birthday. For this I was given a bounty of £200 and a top rate of pay. We invested some £100 of this as a deposit on a car. I became the proud owner of a 1948 Vauxhall Fourteen 6-cylinder saloon, some 12 years old and needing a lot of work done on it.

Even in 1960 few people had cars, preferring to spend money in the mess on entertaining but at that time I smoked very little and drank virtually nothing. But now I spent a lot of cash keeping this car on the road. It was worn out and used about as much oil as petrol. The tyres were worn and the brakes were useless but I

Our first car... Halton, 1959.

was deeply proud of it and it ran reasonably well. We spent the first proper holiday of our married life down at Hayling Island, travelling in this monster. It was a big car by the standard of cars in those days and it gave us the freedom of choice, which was always limited by rail travel. Unfortunately the driving shaft, universal joints went u/s on the journey and it cost me nearly all my spare cash to fix them at a local garage. Yes, we took risks in those days but then any little pleasure was so welcome after the years of being so totally hard up. We greatly enjoyed the holiday; it was only a week but we went down again that same year, using the same little chalet, which had been rented to us by one of the MPBW chaps on the unit. We enjoyed it all but ended very hard up.

I found a lot of pleasure in keeping that car on the road. Motorcycles of the past were interesting but involved only me. If the car was not working, however, then the whole family suffered. Gaining a lot of experience this way enabled me to offer advice to others on the unit who needed help with their broken-down wrecks and I found that I was quite good at fixing cars with problems, so decided to start charging people for the jobs I did. This was taking a bit of a risk but it was worth it as it brought me in a few extra pounds. One week in particular (and one must remember, I am speaking of 1960 when my pay was only some £20 per week) netted me an extra £11. This was a fortune. So we began to live a bit more comfortably but I had to be careful, as the RAF was not keen on servicemen making money on the side.

One of the other problems was the state of one's hands when working on oily cars and then working in the daytime in the operating theatre, where oily hands and fingernails were not approved of. So I had to find methods of keeping my hands clean and spent a lot of time scrubbing and anointing my hands with all kinds of ointments to keep them as fresh as possible. Even so at times I ended up with very sore hands indeed.

I enjoyed the comparative opulence of my illegal work for some five years and had refined it to the point where I regularly serviced cars of various medical officers and the Princess Mary's sisters. My special attraction to these people, in those days before courtesy cars became common to garages, was to loan the customer my car to use in an emergency while I repaired or serviced theirs. This attracted quite a lot of people and by the time I was posted out, I had an extra income of at least £40 per month, which all helped in bringing up a young family. My own car, in the meantime, continued to run but not quite so well now, as I spent more time working on other people's cars. At least it never really let me down.

As comfortable as we were in the job and in other ways, I began to get itchy feet and after the baby was born, I decided I should really begin to look to the future professionally and get other experience. I conveyed my feelings to the Air Commodore, who said he would be sorry to see me leave. But I had had five years of experience in anaesthetics and theatre work and needed to progress. He asked me where I would like to go and I said Changi, Singapore.

Singapore at the time was one of the plum postings of the RAF. It was a three-year tour and most people did well financially out of this type of posting. It was also in the tropics and I would be looking after a new type of patient as well as experiencing foreign travel with the family. Yes, he would arrange this, he said. He came back some three weeks later and said Changi was full; would Cyprus be all right? It sounded great.

Another month went by and one day I was told to get my yellow fever injection and other inoculations organised, as I was going to Gan in the Maldive Islands. This really took the wind out of my sails. Gan was an unaccompanied, one-year posting to what was basically a desert island in the Indian Ocean. It was a posting that was feared by most people, almost a punishment posting. But that was that; I had no option but to comply. When I arrived home to tell my wife, she was, to say the least, annoyed, saying 'This is all the reward you get for working hard'. Unfortunately, this was nothing of the sort but a routine posting, and as I had had eight years in the Air Force without an overseas posting and everyone else was going abroad every two years, I could not really complain. However, with three young children, my wife was now to be left high and dry in six months' time. Of course she was not allowed to stay in the quarter, but was offered a quarter down in Southampton, which was the old RAF sea plane base at Calshot.

This was not an enviable prospect, so I asked her parents if she could go and live with them for a year while I was away. They accepted but my wife was not happy with the idea. However, we all had to put up or shut up. Unfortunately my wife caught german measles, then the flu, and things went from bad to worse. The new baby had persistent bronchitis and by Christmas we were in a state of despair and I was due to take myself off again.

Once again on January 4th (an inauspicious day this seems to be) I was to go off to Lyneham for my journey to Gan – not a happy time. We now had to sort out our belongings again, some going into store, which the RAF paid for. Then we had to decide what would go to the in-laws, which was not much. My beloved car, of course, had to go; there was nowhere to store it so I advertised it and only had one offer. This was from one of the senior NCOs, a recently qualified SRN, who wanted it for his son. He offered me £50 for it and I accepted as I had no better offer. He lived out at Luton and it was arranged that on the way to the in-laws at Henlow, I would call in on him and leave him the car. He would pay me and then he would run my family and me over to the in-laws in his own car. However, when we arrived at his house on a cold January day, he told me that his son hadn't been to the bank that day so he hadn't got any money. He would send it to me. And that was the last I ever saw of it. Numerous letters went unanswered and the RAF wouldn't help: another lesson learned, I'm afraid. It was a great disappointment, as in 1963 £50 was a lot of money and I could ill afford its loss. Still, my wife and children settled down into life at Henlow and on 3rd January I said goodbye and took the train to Lyneham for posting to Gan.

CHAPTER FIVE

The Far East

I arrived at RAF Lyneham at midday and was duly processed for the journey to the Far East. Unfortunately we were forced to wait around at the unit as it was not certain which aircraft we would be travelling on. In those days the new Comet 4 had just come into service. It was the last word in passenger air transport and could travel at about 500 miles per hour at 35,000 feet, so even though Gan was some 8,000 miles away, it was not to be an arduous journey. However the other aircraft were Bristol Britannias, which were turbo props and a lot slower. Besides, they carried fewer passengers and took about an extra 10 hours of flight for the journey.

One of the chaps who was going to Gan was a chief technician air-frame fitter. Dave was a West of England man from Plymouth. He had a lovely West of England burr to his voice and often referred to my family and my new daughter as your little maid. Dave was naturally very well informed about aircraft and movements of aircraft and he gave me a lot of information about this side of the Royal Air Force. We stayed in the transit mess for some four days until the flight was arranged. Happily we were to travel in the RAF executive Comet 4, which was taking the RAF Chaplain-in-Chief on a tour of the Far East Units. It had been snowing heavily that winter in 1963 and we had not seen the sun for some days. So the prospect of palm trees and coral beaches was most appealing.

The time came, after our processing, for us to board the VIP Comet at 1700 hours and we found ourselves in the rear cabin, with 42 seats, in this lovely new jet aircraft. I had never flown in a jet aircraft before and will always remember the massive acceleration as we hurtled down the runway between great banks

Gan in the Maldive Islands... The nearest island is called Fedhu.

of snow and suddenly up into the cloud and through it into the setting sun above rank upon rank of grey cloud below. As the sun set, we settled down to a standard RAF meal of cold meat and salad and made ourselves comfortable for the next four hours until we landed in Libya at El Adem at about 2200 hours local time. Once again it was a further great experience to leave the aircraft and venture into the warm, desert-scented night, where everything smelt burnt and mysterious.

I always remember that as we waited outside the transit mess while the aircraft was refuelled, we were watching a beetle pushing a lump of dung along the concrete path! Looking around me, all I could see was sand – no trees or any other distinguishing features apart from the buildings. My initial thoughts were 'What a place! Fancy being posted here!' Little did I know that some three years later I would be posted there and have to put up with it, and that indeed it would be a very happy posting.

We took off again about 11 p.m. I settled down for the night and when I awoke we were on our final approach to Aden. We banked over the ragged rocky hills of Crater before landing in the

THE FAR EAST

brilliant morning sun at 0500 hours local time. Then we looked around at this big desert town; my feelings were much the same as before ... what a place! But after a good breakfast of bacon and tinned tomatoes, a standard RAF breakfast, we felt more comfortable and were bussed back to the aircraft for the last lap.

We left eventually at 10.30 local time and flew over the Horn of Africa – quite a sight! For somebody like me it was a revelation to view this heat-tortured land from 35,000 feet. We eventually arrived at Gan at about 1500 hours local time after a total flying time of some 15 hours. This was quite a good journey; in 1998 this same journey took me 22 hours, but then it is a different world today.

Better to travel hopefully than to arrive! I had always believed in this saying so I didn't want to get off the plane. However, we emerged into another world smelling of the sea and other indefinable scents that I had never experienced before. The runway took up the whole centre of the island, which was some 2 miles long by 1½ miles wide. The place was organised just like any other RAF unit at home, with tidy gardens and buildings, immaculate roads, street lighting and all round the edge, bright green palm trees standing by white beaches and the most beautiful blue sea with the most lovely cloudless sky overhead. It didn't feel too hot either. The constant wind kept it cool at a temperature of about 80 degrees f. day and night.

The bus took us up to the domestic area and we were all allocated our living accommodation. I was amazed at what I found. Before I came here I had asked several people who had done a year on the island about it all. Some said it was all right; some, when asked about the topography, couldn't remember if there were any trees or what features there were; some said it stank from the smell of fish, others could only comment upon the fact that the island had 13 bars; and some had only noticed the golf course. So it was quite an experience to arrive in this beautiful hot tropical island, just south of the equator, to find myself surrounded by all the 'mod. cons.' of the usual service establishments and to find oneself surrounded by sheer beauty. In those days, however, the only people who had air conditioning in their rooms were the aircrew. However, we soon got used to the heat.

I was met by the member of the sick quarters staff whom I was replacing and shown the ropes. After a heavy night in the mess, I went to sleep totally exhausted until awoken at 0600 hours by my colleague to start work in sick quarters at 0700 hours that morning. I was still unaccustomed to the khaki drill uniform and sandals on my feet. Gan is one of the islands of Addu Atoll. The whole atoll was some 12 miles long and 10 miles across, spread around a blue lagoon. Gan was the most northerly of the islands. We were separated from the other islands by a channel. Gan had been used during the War as a seaplane base and refuelling depot for the Royal Navy. It was reactivated about 1957, as part of the global Commonwealth Defence Organisation, as a refuelling stop for aircraft on their way to and from the Far East. It was a vital part also of the radio communication system for the Armed Forces. It had two big transmitters built on the largest island of the group, called Hittadu. There were no satellites in position then, so to have bases right around the world like this every two to three thousand miles was essential in order to maintain contact with forces that were then deployed in so many regions of the world. With the arrival of the satellite communication system, many of these bases were closed and in 1975 Gan itself closed, reopening in 1992 as a civilian holiday island.

The total native population of Gan consisted of some 2,000 souls at the time of the beginning of our tenancy. They had been moved off the island with the authority of the main government, whose headquarters were in Male some 400 miles to the north. The Maldive Islands, of which Addu Atoll was part, had been a British Protectorate since Victorian times and was now under the rather undemocratic control of the Sultan, who lived in Male in a large palace. But there had been a palace revolution just before I arrived, and the new government was supposedly democratic, having deposed the Sultan, and was rather left wing, with leanings towards the Eastern Block. However, the British government maintained reasonable relations with it for the sake of convenience. It helped to add to our defence commitment worldwide and our government did all it could to avoid trouble. As part of this arrangement, the native population of Addu Atoll, who were of Indian extraction, were to be cared for medically by the RAF medical services. However, they had to visit Gan for treatment as no British airman was allowed to visit the other islands in the atoll apart from the monthly visit by the RAF hygiene squads to dis-infect water sources and generally look after public sanitation.

It was very much Third World in the islands, and the people were very poor by our standards, living mainly off fish and coconuts. The main exports of fish and copra and other forms of general trading with the rest of the archipelago had been suspended by the northern government as part of their disagreement with us. And the local leaders of Addu Atoll had attempted to declare UDI and had formed their own trading company and even a bank. This had been achieved under the astute eye of the senior local politician, named Affi Didi, and it caused us a lot of embarrassment. So the RAF were in an isolated situation. However, with a Royal Navy warship in the vicinity or refuelling in the lagoon and various aircraft bombers and fighters continually flying through, peace was maintained. Once or twice the northern government attempted to assert themselves politically and sent their representatives to the atoll for talks. They were thrown out by the locals after a number of riots and when a squadron of the RAF Regiment arrived, peace was restored again and the men from Male were escorted back to their boats and sent packing.

Our job, then, was to look after some 500 RAF personnel and then care for the islanders, whose general health was of a low standard due to poor diet and various infestations with parasites, worms and allergic conditions. Connected with these were anaemia, various conditions common to all under-nourished people, vitamin deficiency and the usual injuries. One of the great scourges was filariasis, a parasitic invasion of a worm that migrated from the stomach to the lungs and then to the lymphatics, causing massive swelling of the legs and, in men, of the scrotum. This bug was spread by various factors, mainly mosquitoes in the environment, and they had no means of coping with it up till the arrival of the RAF.

So into this virgin medical territory I was now dropped and I had a lot of learning to do. On the first Friday morning at 0700 hours I reported to the Senior Medical Officer, Wing Commander Facer. He was one of the anaesthetists I had met at Halton while I was working for the Air Commodore. The SMOs, because they were going to Gan, were given a course in anaesthetics before posting, but there was much surgery to do on the islands, mainly on the natives. The Junior Medical Officer was actually a trainee surgeon who was gaining the experience for his fellowship at The Royal College of Surgeons. This type of work was invaluable to young surgeons. I got on very well with the Wing Commander at Halton and was able to be a lot of help to him in Gan, as I knew the anaesthetic system inside out. I spent a lot of my time in the operating theatre assisting him while he did the anaesthetics.

The senior NCO in charge of the sick quarters was rather a fat and pompous flight sergeant who was unmarried and objected volubly to married personnel getting an enhanced overseas allowance; it was more than he was getting. He went out of his way to be offensive but he was the boss and I had no option but to do what he said. As I spent a lot of my time in the theatre, he couldn't get at me as much as he would have liked.

My other task was to look after two 8-bedded airmen's wards and an air-conditioned ward in which we put our patients who were suffering from sunstroke and prickly heat. This work didn't take a lot of effort, but we were usually full of patients with cuts from the coral, incurred when swimming, and also with gut upsets, often from too much drinking. This was, for the majority of the people, the only way to avoid boredom. A lot of people did feel bored and many were resentful because for some reason they felt it was a punishment posting and made the worst of it.

However, because the SMO knew of my previous experience in

plastic surgery, my other role was to look after the patients who had some skin loss due to accidents with corrosives or other substances they had not met before. A number of the natives on the island were used as waiters in the mess and general assistants to other services, such as the maintenance staff and sanitation people. Sometimes they brought substances back to the islands at night if they thought they might be useful to themselves. Some of the resulting accidents were horrendous. I remember one young 12 year-old girl who was terribly burned about the legs due to a petrol fire. The emergency lamps on the runways were called goosenecks. They were filled with kerosene and were used if the runway lights failed due to a power station breakdown. These were often found to be empty by the staff who maintained the airfield in the morning. It was discovered that it was because the natives would empty them at night and take the kerosene back to the islands for their own lamps. The Maldivian lamp usually held palm oil and was like an ancient Roman lamp; it was a saucer held up by four pieces of coconut twine and tied to a rafter immediately inside the hut. Kerosene, of course, gave them far better light than palm oil.

Realising what was happening, some idiot put aviation spirit into the goosenecks to teach the natives a lesson. When the lamp was lit, the flames would flare up, burn the cord and the lamp would fall to the floor and explode, causing massive burns to anyone near. This would usually be the children.

So the young girl was brought in and although she did not appear too badly burned on the legs to the casual observer, it was very difficult to tell on a dark skin. Being experienced in burns, I realized that she had full thickness burns on both legs to above the knee. She had no pain because the burn was so deep. These were simple people who did not complain unless they could see injury. Straightaway I gave her a sedative and prepared to dress these wounds with paraffin gauze and saline packs, as was the usual treatment in those days. It was very hard work, trying to explain to the relatives and keeping them out of the way. About 15 minutes after bandaging, the child's temperature began to soar and I realised that she was getting heat-stroke. I asked the SMO if we could put her in a room on her own so that we could expose the wounds and just irrigate them in an aseptic atmosphere. One of the Maldivian nursing attendants, of whom we had about three, was given the task of cleaning out a room so that we could do this. I told him to get cracking but he refused and laughed at me. I didn't understand that so I shouted at him but he still wouldn't do it and continued to laugh, so I had to do it myself. The SMO told me afterwards that in his eyes cleaning out rooms was women's work and not his. The fact that he was laughing showed he was embarrassed. A steep learning curve was going to be needed, I could see.

So, the room was prepared and we put her in and linked her to a normal saline drip. Then we started work on her night and day for 14 days. By the end of this time all the dead tissue had sloughed off and she was being treated with high protein foods and fluids by the drip. However, it was exceedingly difficult to make this almost stone-age child understand what needed to be done to save her life. She was progressing well, or so I thought, and almost ready for skin grafting. One night as I was going to sleep one of the nursing attendants came running over to my room and called me to see the girl. She had got out of bed and was walking around the room crying. I rushed over. She was totally demented and running around. She pulled out her drip, removed all the equipment and kept screaming. I sedated her with a powerful sedative, redressed all I could and repositioned the drip. She eventually settled down to sleep.

The next morning as I went into the sick quarters, I heard a lot of shouting going on. Her relatives had forced the door and she was lying dead on the floor. She had had a massive pulmonary embolus. It was difficult to help these people by treating them with European methods and I realise now that we were wrong to do it. But morally speaking what else could we do?

This episode shook me deeply but the work had to go on. It was often heartbreaking to see our failures, but then we had so many more successes. These little people were as tough as old boots and so grateful for what we did for them. Then too, after all, we had the resources and they had even less than nothing, if that were possible.

One sad incident occurred some months later. A little 3 year-old boy was admitted unconscious and after blood tests we found he was a diabetic. He had a massive blood sugar level and we spent all morning bringing the level down. He recovered consciousness about 1200 hours and appeared to be reasonably stable after massive injections of insulin and glucose. I told the nursing attendant that I was going to the mess for lunch and left the child with him and his father. When I returned 20 minutes later, the nursing attendant and the boy's father were playing cards on the floor at the foot of the bed and the child was dead. My reaction was one of extreme anger and I kicked them both out of the sick quarters, shouting threats at them. The SMO came out of his office to see what the noise was. I told him the story and he took me into his office. Then he said this to me:

'Sergeant, we had to do that. We were morally bound to resuscitate him but this is really the best way.'

Where would he have got insulin? Would his parents have used it? What about a diabetic diet and what about all the other care he needed? Could they possibly understand? We were in the Third World, not the UK. I then realised another fact of life here. How lucky we were to live in the West and that we had, thanks to our own volition, a good medical service, social service and all the trappings of civilisation, which they had not and which they would not have for many years. It has taken us a thousand years to get where we are today, and even now we often fail and are not satisfied.

So life was full of interests, surprises and disappointments, but professionally I was learning a lot. The European problems were mainly due to accidents, horseplay and injudicious behaviour. Coral cuts were sometimes quite dramatic and needed very special attention. The conventional method of treatment did not seem to apply. The cuts were infected and although they were cleaned well aseptically, they often didn't heal. This was one of the greatest

Author in ill-fitting khaki drill before a flight in the station helicopter.

problems for fair-skinned people in the tropics. Any swimming was dangerous unless one wore goggles and could see under the water, because the number of coral heads even in shallow water was quite considerable.

Coral is, of course, a skeleton case made of chalk which contains a small coral animal, so any cut was contaminated by the protein in the coral creature, which appeared to impart an allergic reaction over and above the trauma of the cut. When I arrived on the island, many of the staff were suffering from heavily infected cuts which had not healed and were now shallow ulcers and, although they had been dressed daily with the usual treatments available, such as antibiotic cream and sterile dressings, they could take 6–8 months to heal. It destroyed the men's pleasure in swimming, one of the great pleasures here for most of the airmen.

I asked the SMO if I could experiment a little and devise some treatments which might speed up the healing process. My first approach was to consider the effect of antibiotics on the skin and I realised that in using these, we were also destroying the common bacteria which live normally on the skin and seem to keep the skin healthy and in good condition. So I started by treating the ulcers with daily cleaning, application of Vaseline gauze and normal saline dressing, removing the debris each day and keeping the area clean. It had quite a dramatic effect and after a week or so these ulcers began to heal. Almost without exception, the whole procedure then went into reverse and by the end of the second week they were absolutely back to square one, but at least they were not now infected. All the new skin that had grown had disappeared. Thinking this through, I came to the conclusion that it was because although the skin was now clean, the pH of the skin and the occlusive dressing in a hot, damp and sweaty climate were militating against healing. The next idea was to expose the wound to the sun for a limited time each day to let the ultra-violet light work on it and to cover it at night. This only attracted flies. Then I covered the wound with cellophane and put that in the sun. For some reason the wound became infected again. This was proving to be a nightmare.

Nobody else had any ideas so I tried once more. This time I flushed out the ulcer with normal saline, puffed a very small amount of sulpha powder on it, and, to the great discomfort of the patients, sprayed it over with Nobecutane, a kind of liquid skin. The area was then exposed to the air and to the sun for an hour a day. Two days later it was obvious that this was working. By peeling off the liquid skin, repeating the process three times a week, the ulcers healed from the outside in. Thereafter this became the standard treatment whilst I was on the island and made a great contribution to the health of the chaps.

Another problem was sea urchins. The unwary would swim without flippers or shoes and tread on these wretched things. The spine of the urchin would penetrate the skin of the foot to the depth of ½ inch at a time, causing great pain, and it was very difficult to remove. We had to open the entrance of the wound with a scalpel and if we couldn't grasp the spine with forceps and pull it out, a dressing of magnesium sulphate had to be applied to the spine and it would be drawn out by the hydroscopic dressing.

The greatest danger of the sandy beaches and shallow waters, however, was the stonefish, which buried itself into the seabed with only the spine showing above the sand. The spines were only about 6 to 8 cms long but the puncture wound and the injection of the toxin were invariably totally disabling due to the resulting excruciating pain, which was not eased even by morphine. Fortunately this was a rare occurrence and I only saw one case. Luckily the spine had only scratched the skin. But the reaction of the patient, the swelling of his foot and his immense pain had to be seen to be believed. He required very heavy doses of morphine and anti-histamines to resolve the problem, and he was in bad shape for about a fortnight and very weak for some time afterwards.

The sea was quite a dangerous place and although we were often warned about its dangers, we had only one fatality. A young navy diver on an exercise on the lagoon was lost some 120 feet down. His instructor, who should have stuck to him like a leech, for some reason came up to the surface to locate his position and on returning to the seabed couldn't find the trainee. It was about two hours before he was found by the other divers. By this time his air had run out and he was beyond help. They brought him ashore and we took him straight to the operating theatre, where we intubated him, put him on a drip and tried to get his heart started again by direct cardiac-massage through the chest wall. After two hours, although he had shown some response, the surgeon had to stop as he was getting nowhere and the patient was now brain dead.

The poor chap was buried at sea two days later off the atoll in 6,000 feet of water. The RAF padre told me it was a very moving ceremony. There was absolute silence at the committal. He was so used to sounds when burying the dead on land, as cars went by in the distance and people talked in the cemetery, that this burial struck him as eerily silent. After it, the lad's effects were auctioned and I was surprised by the generosity of the crew of the destroyer. They raised about £1,300 for his bits and pieces, which were really not worth much at all, and sent this to his widowed mother in the north.

But life was not all work. We did work hard and we played hard: football, tennis, cricket and so on. There was also a nine-hole golf course laid out on one side of the runway which kept the golfers happy. A lot of men went fishing, which was very popular; many varieties of fish were seen and caught. One chap caught a couple of sharks. They were only small creatures and we put them in the static water tank near the main communications centre. They were about $3^1/_2$ feet long but it was most eerie when you walked to the tanks and these sharks hurtled towards you eyeing you with quite a degree of malevolence. They lived there quite happily for the last four months of my tour on the island, but I would have thought that their demise was imminent due to the unchanged water in the tank and the fact that not a lot of people remembered to feed them.

The other great sport was snorkelling. Everybody tried it who was posted here and when I arrived, my skills at swimming were about nil. I seemed to have the ability to sink to the bottom without really trying. I was persuaded by a colleague to get some flippers and a face mask and found I took to it literally like a fish to water. I spent many a happy hour in my off duty swimming over the reef. I had seen television films of the life of a reef which had been made by naturalists Hans and Lottie Haas, but in those days such films were in black and white. Suddenly there was this fabulous underwater garden and brightly coloured fish to explore and I was fascinated to be part of it. Scuba diving had hardly made an impact as yet. Commander Cousteau of the French Navy had made it popular but it cost a lot of money for the equipment and it was new and experimental, so I never did have a go at it. Snorkelling, however, was great fun for me in water over the reef, which was usually no more than 5 to 10 feet deep. We could spend hours looking at the fish. We indulged in horse-play at these times; being young and rather foolish, one of our great games was to play submarines and destroyers. The destroyer (your mate of course) had a couple of depth charges available to sink you, the submarine. The depth charges were empty lager tins which, when filled with water, would crash into the sea with a very satisfying thud and hopefully miss the submarine. However one day, one hit me on the head with a resounding crack and suddenly the sea in my immediate area was full of my blood. The first thought that came into my mind was sharks and I raced for the shore about 30 yards away like a young torpedo. My colleague, the destroyer, followed me laughing until we arrived at the beach and he looked at my scalp. He then had to stitch up the wound to stop the bleeding but really it was good fun and no bad feelings were evinced.

My next venture earned me quite a lot of notoriety. I was, of course, quite well known amongst the men for my work in sick quarters and the mess was aware of how hard we worked there. In fact we were quite well thought of. One day at the weekly mess meeting the CMC, a Warrant Officer Jones (I met a lot of Warrant Officer Jones's in the Air Force), asked for a volunteer to look after the caged birds which lived in the small aviary on the lawn behind the mess. These birds, a couple of parakeets, cockatoos and zebra finches and a host of budgerigars, were looked after by a sergeant who worked in the stores while the mess paid for the food. But the sergeant was due to be posted home in a month and a replacement was needed. The CMC asked for volunteers and as usual nobody wanted the trouble. After two appeals, the CMC said that if no volunteers came forward, the birds would have to be put down. However, the birds gave a lot of pleasure and were well known to the visiting aircrew, who had taught the parakeet to swear like a trooper. Its comment when anyone went to look into the cage or to give them a couple of biscuits or some currants was 'F off' repeated again and again.

The CO had decided that there were not enough people to

perform station duties, so even the sick quarter staff would have to take their part. I thought this was unfair as we were already on duty nearly every other day and on duty for all emergencies. We had quiet periods only occasionally and I expressed my annoyance to the SMO, who said there was nothing he could do about it; this was just one of those things. Thinking this over in my mind one morning, I just happened to be talking to the Warrant Officer in his office and brought up the subject of the birds. He agreed that it was a shame but said he would have to get rid of them next week. I replied by saying that I was really busy and now with the extra duties he proposed, I would have no spare time or I would do it. Straight away he said, 'if you do it, boy, you don't need to do station duties.' So now I became the birdman of Gan as well. It didn't take too much effort. I emptied the sand trays at the bottom of the aviaries daily and put down the shutters at night, emptied the trays onto the beach and replaced the old litter with fresh clean sand every day. After a couple of weeks or so, the RAF police came to see me and asked me what I was growing on the beach where I emptied the trays. We had had a couple of wet days or so and some of the seeds were growing rapidly. One of the policemen recognised them as cannabis; apparently the birdseed imported by the NAAFI contained hemp seed. I had to be a little more careful and emptied the trays into the sea in future. I thought the police looked at me rather strangely.

I didn't really like looking after the birds. However it was better than station duties and indeed they were a source of very real pleasure to the men. But one day I noticed that the birds were getting very agitated at night when I pulled the shutters down. Then the numbers of the small birds began to drop and one morning I found a severed head from one of the budgerigars on the floor of the cage. There was no evidence of vermin on the island. It appeared to be free of rodents, and when I asked the hygiene section about this, I was told there were only a few palm rats, which were vegetarian, and the landcrabs, which couldn't climb as high as that. After a week or so I had lost over half of the birds but one afternoon a line squall was approaching the island at some 40 knots and the tannoy told us to bring down all shutters and curtains in the offices and departments. There was a curtain on the birds' aviary which I had never let down as it didn't cover much but I ran up from sick quarters and let this one down along with the others so as to protect the birds from the soaking. When we had a line squall, the rain pelted horizontally with great force. So I let the bamboo curtain down and as it unrolled, three large rats fell out. They had built a nest in the rolled up curtain. I and a colleague managed to catch them all and we killed them and took them to the hygiene section. The hygienist opened them up and we found their guts to be full of feathers and beaks, so our vegetarian rats had proved to be carnivorous after all.

Time passed and it was now October. The weather was getting dry with only the occasional shower. Christmas was approaching and I had had a fortnight's leave in Singapore in September with my friend, where I had bought a lot of things to take home to the family. By now I was looking forward to January in the UK again. My two weeks in Singapore had gone quickly and it had been a most enjoyable experience, although I was nearly eaten alive by mosquitoes. The only unpleasantness occurred when my colleague and I went to the airfield at RAF Changi for the journey back to Gan at the end of the holiday. We presented ourselves, only to be told to go and get our uniforms on as we couldn't travel in an RAF transport aircraft in civvies. We had, of course, come to Changi in civvies in an RAF Transport Command aircraft so we had none with us. The flight sergeant was quite officious and overbearing and refused to accept us on the flight. 'OK,' I said, 'I will sit here and you will have to see our CO at Gan and tell him we can't return. 'He went inside to get a civilian civil servant, who was a good deal less than civil. He told us to stand up when we talked to him. When we didn't stand up, he became upset. He repeated his mission statement; it really didn't worry us. I would have stayed on for at least another month in Singapore; it was a plum posting in those days. After a lot of arguing and close

An Avro Hastings long-range transport on arrival from Singapore via Colombo.

studying of our travel documents, they had to do something and we were grudgingly allowed to board an old Hastings transport which took 12 hours to Gan via Colombo, where we stayed in the mess for the night before flying down to Gan the next day.

As it was nearly Christmas, we were already practising in the chapel for the carol service. We had a very good organist, a Welshman who played in his chapel at home. There was also a Welsh meteorological officer who had a good tenor voice. One of the hygiene section corporals was a counter-tenor – remarkable to find one on an island in the Indian Ocean; they are very rare. I sang tenor, we had a couple of basses, so we did quite well. My short incumbency as the regular organist had given me a lot of pleasure also. To be away from the family for a year was hard to bear, although everyone was in the same boat, but the chaplain of the church was a great source of comfort. I had always had a leaning towards the C of E and this really cemented my ideas; I realised that this formal form of worship and protocol was to me very comforting. Most RAF padres, when you got to know them, were good men and worked very hard. They took a lot of flack from the men but stood up well to it all and made a huge contribution to the running of the unit. The chaplain was a social worker as well as pastor and it needed an officer's rank to help deflect some of the obvious unfairness that was sometimes meted out to the lower orders from the higher ones.

We had a very active little church and we had the usual services: matins, evensong and eucharist and bible study every Tuesday evening, at which a group of eight to ten of us were often present and where many a lively discussion was held on spiritual matters. Evenings were a good time for this, and we usually ended at about 10 p.m. with the little service of compline, which was an excellent way to end the evening. The church club was at the other end of the chapel and we had other functions there, such as a music circle and the occasional visit from any of the VIPs who were interested enough to come and talk to us. I remember one visitor, a retired brigadier accompanied by his wife. He was a famous round-the-world sailor and he gave us a couple of excellent accounts of his various adventures. The next day the padre was invited on board the Brigadier's yacht for lunch. The Brigadier and his wife were a charming couple. The padre told me afterwards that it was very hot in the cabin and the Brigadier's good lady was serving a cold collation, as she put it. As she opened the tin of sardines, the sweat was dropping off her nose all over the sardines on his plate. He said that he felt distinctly that he went pale and had to go up on deck for air!

Another VIP who visited us was Hammond Innes, who was collecting information for his book *The Strode Adventurer*. I spent a morning with him in the helicopter as we flew around the atoll. He was a most friendly and interesting man and his subsequent book showed that he had genuinely done his homework. Another of his books, *A Harvest of Islands*, delved very deeply into the politics of the area and made highly interesting reading for me on my return home. We were really unaware of all the wheeling and dealing that was going on between the various governments and departments involved during our time there.

It was now November and our SMO, Wing Commander Facer,

THE FAR EAST

was due to be replaced by another SMO of the same rank. We had a very gentle farewell party in the hospital and I for one was very sorry to see him go. He had been a good boss and a very considerate and astute officer, who always listened to anything you had to say. He respected the views of his staff and acknowledged the expertise of whatever grade of staff he had working for him. His replacement was a small man of about 5'4", in contrast to the Wing Commander, who was 6', but he had a different personality, hailed from somewhere in Scotland, and really didn't suffer fools gladly. Even for him the learning curve was steep. This really was a different sort of work and we all had to adapt to a different set of circumstances, including the heat. He had done a short course in anaesthetics at Halton before his posting and, with my experience of both Halton and Gan and also my knowledge of the local set up, I was able to be very useful to him. We seemed to hit it off straight away.

On his first full morning he told me to come and join him in his surgery to help him with the sick parade and identify what he termed the scroungers and skivers. We started at 7.00 a.m. with the usual list of aches and pains and gut problems and so on, coral cuts and dental problems. As we had no resident dentist, I did simple dentistry, having had some tuition from a dental officer passing through on his way to Singapore . . . but more of that later. At a certain point a young man appeared who was very smarmy and a bit of a smart Alec. The SMO asked him what his problem was as he stood before him. Leaning forward with his fingers resting on the SMO's desk, the chap replied that he had a problem with constipation. The SMO looked at him and said,

'Well, that's not worrying me, lad, it's your legs, isn't it lad?' And he turned to me and said, 'What do you think of his legs, Sergeant?' So obviously playing the game, I went round to the other side of the desk and looked at him. Then I said,

'Oh dear!'

'Quite so!' said the SMO, 'Your legs!'

The poor chap, looking wholly confused, glanced up and said, 'But there is nothing wrong with my legs, Sir.'

'Well,' said the SMO, 'Bloody stand on them then when you come in here to see me in future!'

'Oh dear', I thought, 'this is what we have got to put up with, is it?' However, he proved to be a good man for all that and a very hard worker.

His junior medical officer, the surgeon, was a rather tall gangling individual who wanted to do good to everyone, especially if the patient was a native. He felt that we were exploiting the native people and seemed to have no concept of what the Third World was all about. He requested permission from the new senior medical officer to start training a few native midwives in modern methods in order to cut the number of obstetric complications and abortions which occurred, and which in fact kept the population at a sustainable level. This was a very hard thing for an idealistic Western-trained person to appreciate but it was a fact of life. So he ordered quite a lot of equipment, including stethoscopes, foetal heart stethoscopes and so on, notebooks and pens and all the usual things needed for the average student, nor would he take 'no' for an answer.

Our medical assistant, Mr Don Tutu, a native who spoke good English, kept reminding him that this would not work because ... etc. etc. But the doctor knew what he was doing and asked Don Tutu to get the midwives, one from each island, to attend the hospital for instruction in the form of a series of six weekly lectures. Now, the midwives were all elderly and respected by the locals, in fact invaluable members of their communities. What they had learned derived from experience over the years and also from a lot of local folklore which was included in this experience. As is the norm in these basic societies, much knowledge was passed on by word of mouth. When the great day arrived and all the midwives were present, Don Tutu acted as interpreter. They were all issued with their kits, which included the items mentioned previously plus urinary-testing kits and so on. The junior medical officer started lecturing, using the newly purchased blackboard and charts, which he had obtained from MOD. After ten minutes he realised that this rather unenthusiastic audience of midwives was not taking any notes or paying much attention and he asked Don Tutu what the problem was.

'I've been trying to tell you, Sir,' he said, 'They can't read or write and they don't know why they are here.'

So that was the end of that. I don't know how much it must have cost. I was sometimes surprised at the way the native women did trust us, however. They would often arrive at midnight and be brought in on their beds by either a husband or a mother, having been in labour for some days. Most were very dehydrated, fully dilated, but with no movement. On being questioned, they would tell you what they thought you wanted to know. They would tell you that they were maybe 12 months pregnant and had been in labour for two weeks. Often a simple answer would be a couple of

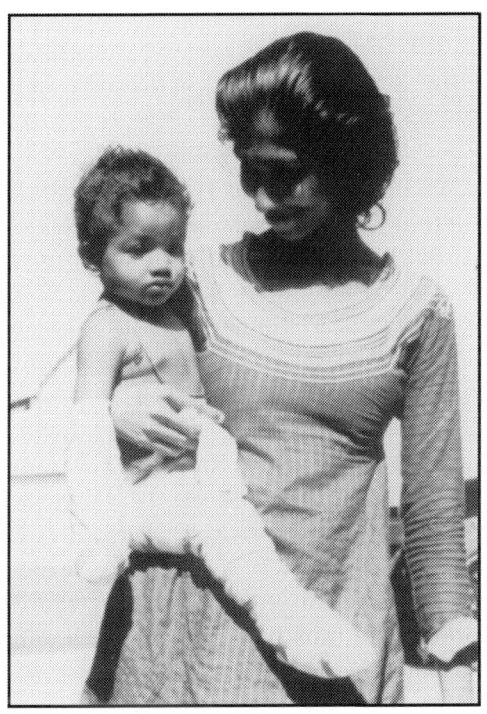

Young native patient with serious burns in the arms of his mother.

suppositories, and the baby would arrive on the way home. The average mother was only about 17 or 18 years old. They started child-bearing at about the age of 12. One of the first caesarean sections I helped with was on a young girl of 13 whom we delivered of twins. These teenage mothers had no problem with pushing out their babies, and then about an hour later, after a rest, they would go back to their housework or whatever they usually did. They had few inhibitions. They would shout and bawl while in labour and 'do their own thing', but in three months they would be pregnant again. They looked old at the age of 35 and were often worn out, general health not being good; most had gut infestations; very few had what we in the West would consider to be a good blood picture, due mainly to their poor diet. However, as I noted before, this did keep the population down and there were many miscarriages and infant mortalities. But by the time we left the islands in 1975, things were improving considerably and a new generation that had rubbed shoulders with the West was now in charge. The population was expanding at an alarming rate, so that the British government now had to subsidise their food with meat and rice. Meanwhile the local economy, which was always bedevilled by the refusal of the northern government to allow them to trade, depended to a large extent on the RAF.

I was now due to return home in a month's time and I had a lot of work to do. We had quite a number of people with dental problems, which I used to treat a little. The SMO had asked me, when I arrived, if I had any dental experience. I replied that many years before my brother had been a dental technician. 'That's good enough,' he said, 'You're the dentist.' There were a number of books in the library and I found that most patients' problems were due to dental caries, and that the only course to take in such cases was to take the tooth out. That was the SMO's job under general anaesthetic. Alternatively, I would drill a hole in the top of the tooth, scrape out the contents and fill it with zinc oxide and oil of cloves. This usually worked satisfactorily but it was pretty 'hairy', as I was not allowed to give injections to dull the pain; that would have been dangerous. I did quite a lot of work there and became quite a dab hand at simple dentistry. I had to warn the patients that I was not a dentist and couldn't use an anaesthetic. If they were in agony it wouldn't matter, I couldn't make it any worse, they said. 'Want to bet?' I would think. But at least I saved them some sleepless nights. I did a filling on the senior medical officer before I got home, so I assumed I did some good work and was getting quite a favourable reputation.

We had an enjoyable Christmas with all the usual fare, turkey and plum pudding, which we ate under the palm trees and which was enjoyed by all.

On Christmas day my special air servicing flight friend told me he was going to sort out one of my colleagues in the mess. This chap's name was Bowyer and he was a Sergeant SRN like myself. He was a real rough diamond, thoroughly disliked by everybody in the mess. He was uncouth and would never buy anybody a drink, and when drunk was utterly crude and unpleasant to everybody. He had few friends and didn't seem to care about his unpopularity but after the Christmas dinner we all went into the bar. After about 10 minutes, when free drinks had been started, Dave asked for silence and announced that as a general token of our appreciation and esteem he was going to award a special gift to Bowyer. 'Will Bob please step forward?' Bowyer told him to 'F off' but was persuaded to step forward anyway.

Dave took him to the veranda of the bar and asked him to look out at the trees. Above the palm trees every night, always confused by the lights around the mess, were flying a number of arctic terns which used to live in the area, beautiful white birds. Dave said to Bowyer, 'Now then, that's what I'm going to give you ... that bird up there!' pointing at the largest of two that were flying around at the time. Bowyer of course replied 'F off' in his usual tactful way, but David persisted and demanded that Bowyer say 'thank you', which he eventually did. So in we all went and about an hour later Dave, to the amusement of the mess, took Bowyer out again and showed him these birds and then reminded him every half an hour until midnight that that was his bird. At midnight Dave said to me, 'Now watch this space.' By this time Bowyer was well into his cups and was taken to the veranda again by Dave. A little unsteadily, Dave said, 'I have forgotten which bird was yours.' Bowyer of course replied, 'F off'. So Dave said, 'Oh come on Bob! Whose tern is that?' pointing at the last bird. 'Mine,' replied Bowyer and at this all the mess, who were by now well into it, shouted, 'We will have a double whiskey each!' or whatever came into their heads and the barman had the chits ready to sign, which Bowyer now had no option but to sign. A good laugh was had by all but next morning Bowyer was a lot poorer and in an awful mood.

I was posted home on January 4th, 1965 in a Britannia of Transport Command, but we were delayed by bad weather at El Adem. It was freezing cold when we arrived at the diversion airfield at RAF Valley at 1400 hours on January 7th (Lyneham was closed by fog). I spent the rest of the day travelling home to Henlow, arriving home at 0600 hours the next morning; back to the bosom of my family. It was a cold dark world after the light and warmth of the tropics, but it was wonderful to be home again. I was posted to the RAF Hospital at Uxbridge but had six weeks to use up my leave getting used to family life again. I had, of course, to re-establish my relationship with my children, who were now 1, 5 and 7 years old; they had almost forgotten me. My daughter greeted me by saying 'Hello, man', and burst into tears. I almost copied her but after a week or so things began to fall into place and, although we were living with in-laws, which was a bit traumatic at times, we survived.

My father-in-law was slowly coming round to my side and beginning to realise that I was becoming quite a reasonably experienced serviceman, as he himself had been and, although I was always a bit of a disappointment to him, I felt it was because I could not play golf and maybe it was because I would not. I could never really see the point of ball games. I took him with me to find a car to get us mobile again. We eventually found an ex-staff car previously owned by Smiths Industries and we became the proud owners of an almost immaculate Austin Westminster, which was large enough for our family of five. I had saved a lot of money in Gan because there was little to spend it on, so we were reasonably well off when I returned to the UK. The leave passed quickly and I presented myself to RAF Hospital, Uxbridge in March to try and fit in with treatment and care of patients with malignant disease. This posting was to have a major impact on my professional life.

CHAPTER SIX

Uxbridge

I booked into the mess one Tuesday afternoon in March and was allocated a room. The unit was one of the oldest in the RAF, situated just outside the main part of Uxbridge town, although the mess itself was quite modern. The surroundings looked pleasant but I viewed it all with a jaundiced eye. Here I was again, away from the family. The next morning I attended the hospital at the northern end of the unit to do my arrival procedure.

The hospital was an old country house with wards and departments added on in a rather ramshackle, haphazard way. The orderly room was helpful. I was, after all, a senior NCO and expected to be treated like one. I had by now been in the service for 12 years so knew the ropes. My arrival chit needed signatures from all the departments, the last two being the Commanding Officer and a matron. The CO was a very nice man; unfortunately he was to die of cancer of the lungs within a few months of my arrival. However, when I marched into the matron's office, to my dismay, I found that she was one of the old-style PMs and one whom I had upset some years previously at Halton when I worked in theatre. She was a ward sister then and was now getting on in years and even more assertive and unpleasant than she had been in 1960. Once again I was told I would do as I was told and obey orders. 'Oh dear! Here we go again,' I thought. I was allocated to the Airmen's Ward which was run by an extremely nice ward sister, a Sister Murrey, who was a good team leader and recognised one's ability even if the matron didn't. She had been briefed by the matron about me and was a bit guarded, but after I had spent a day in the department, she found I was not so bad as I had been portrayed by this harridan of a woman.

I settled into the ward without too much trouble but was soon made aware of the high standards required of nursing staff by the consultant, Vice Air Marshall Sir Peter Dixon. Sir Peter was an Australian who had made his career in the Royal Air Force. He was a very gentle man and had a wonderful way with his patients, who I can say without embarrassment, loved him. He seemed to recognise their needs both physically, mentally and spiritually but anybody who did not fit in with his concept was out. I was acting as a staff nurse at the time. The previous staff nurse, a flight sergeant, had been posted and I worked opposite the ward sister. My relationship with the two junior medical officers was good but I found that there was much to learn.

Not a vast amount was known about cancer or its causes in 1968 and consequently not much could be done. There were a few drugs on the market which helped to shrink tumours, but the side-effects were horrendous and frequently worse than the symptoms of the cancer the patient was suffering from. Actually these side-effects often caused their death. A lot of surgery was performed to remove offending tumours, but this really only put off the inevitable day; most types of treatment did not really prolong life but only extended death. The surgeons were well aware of this and it was difficult to remain optimistic in the face of the inevitable when caring for these patients. If we could extend the survival by one year, we were lucky, but even this required frequent attendances at the out-patient clinics to monitor, and a top-up of their blood level with transfusions. Much of the medicine was mainly palliative but it did give a certain quality of life. The steroids really came into their own here and some wellbeing could be generated by giving quite mild doses of these, but even then side effects were a nuisance.

The patients were young men, or young women on the families ward, and looked upon the medical staff, who were by and large mature men, with great affection and indeed gratitude for any relief. I can recall one afternoon, during the usual major round of the week, when the Air Vice Marshal couldn't do his rounds because of pressure of work and the morale of the patients sank to zero. Just to think that such a god-like figure as an Air Vice Marshal would talk with them was quite a source of wonder to some. We must remember that this was 1968 and people did not have such unrealistic expectations as youngsters have today, mainly due to the fact that nowadays the television and radio talk so much about wonderful breakthroughs in medicine that they often give rise to false hopes anyway. The next time he came, the Air Vice Marshall was late. He came into the office and we discussed the patients. We had a 24-bedded ward and he said that he didn't really have time enough to go in. I said very boldly,

'Well, Sir, the patients will be absolutely devastated if you don't.'

He sighed, looked at me and replied, 'Well I sometimes have to pluck up a lot of courage to see these chaps each week.'

'I know, Sir,' I answered, 'but we also have to live with them.'

He smiled and said, 'Okay let's get on with it.' We could feel the tension of the ward ease just because he went in for the round. He was a remarkable man.

I had been in the post for some three months when the CO and the matron were posted. The CO went to the Westminster Hospital for treatment and the matron, I hoped, to the worst posting she could get. Their replacements were both charming, however. The new CO seemed to understand and kept out of the way, and the matron was an extremely supportive and understanding person. Another sergeant SRN had been posted in and he and I hit it off very well and he felt very much as I did about oncology, i.e. the study of malignant disease. He had had some previous experience.

The RAF was now getting short of Princess Mary's nursing sisters and the matron promoted myself and my colleague Alan to be in joint charge of the Airmen's Ward when Sister Murray left. This was highly appreciated by ourselves and we could now put into operation some of our ideas that had been dismissed as unworkable by the previous administration. The nursing attendants took a little time to adjust to us, so Alan and I had them all in the office and pointed out the obvious. We could do it the easy way or the hard way and we had too much to do with the patients to worry about the behaviour of skiving nineteen year-olds, so they would either knuckle down or be punished. This stopped the rot but we instituted a weekly discussion and a teaching session for all the staff thereafter, and the men felt that they were being taken seriously and so co-operated to the full.

Thus life was getting far more pleasant – plenty of hard work indeed, but it was made easier by the fact that by now I had moved into brand new married quarters, which my wife liked. The children were settled in school and with the pay rises we had, we were now doing quite nicely. I can even recall the pleasure we had when we had a five-week pay cheque. This came to over a £100 a month at the time after stoppages, and in 1970, with no travelling to do or major car expenses, this was a good salary. We were able to buy a fridge, washing machine and other electronic goodies, which made life a lot easier for my wife. My wife had also obtained a post as staff nurse at the local geriatric hospital in Hillingdon and was happy there working part-time. Her duties usually fitted in well with mine and, as I could now arrange my own off duty to suit myself, this was a good move. So all in all life was good and improving daily.

We had two more SRNs posted in and they came to work with my colleague and myself. They were both registered mental nurses and this was useful as it gave us another dimension to our care of the chronically and terminally ill patient, and also to the care of their relatives. Jack Edwards was a corporal, a most gregarious and cheerfully optimistic man, who had five children. He was a parachutist from choice and often did freefall jumps as a sport. He always called me 'Vicar', to my annoyance. Goodness knows why, but we got on well. Jim was a very pleasant Irishman and if I remember rightly, he was an excellent nurse and really enhanced our team. I remembered discussing finances one day with Jack and discovered that he didn't have any insurance, even on his car. I didn't believe him. I suggested that this was a bit irresponsible with his parachuting and his five children but then I said,

'I assume your church would look after you if you were killed.' He looked at me strangely and said,

'What do you mean?'

I replied, 'Well . . . the Catholic church you attend.' He exploded. He didn't attend a church; he was an atheist anyway. I was puzzled and said,

'Why is it, then, that your car is always parked outside the Catholic church on the main road right in the middle of the unit?'

He laughed and explained that he was always pushed for a few bob and couldn't put a lot of petrol in the car and, as he usually ran out of petrol on the hill by the church just when he was going to town, that's where it had to stay until he filled it with a can. So that explained that.

As a registered mental nurse, he was useful in other ways. One of our remits at the hospital was to cover Heathrow and Northolt for escort duties when patients were flown in from overseas. One evening, as I was the only one on duty, I was called to collect a sailor from the medical centre at Heathrow. We drove up by car and went to the reception to collect him. I was invited in and given his notes. Then I was told that he was sitting on a seat waiting for me. I went across to him. He looked all right to me, well dressed, polite, a good looking young man of about 25.

'What is the problem then?' I asked the sister in charge.

'Oh,' she said airily, 'He was a little poorly on the flight from Zurich. That's all.'

His notes were sealed and I couldn't see any details, so I collected him, put him in the car and off we set. As we came to the first roundabout he asked me where we were going. I replied 'Uxbridge Hospital.'

'Can I have a bath when we get there?' he asked.

'Of course,' I replied. As we left the tunnel and turned on to the M4 and came to the next roundabout, he asked me the same question again. I replied as before and each time we came to a turning he asked me again.

'Where are we going? Can I have a bath when we get there?' I was getting a bit fed up with this and it was late so I was relieved when we got to the hospital and I handed him over to the ward master, of whom he asked the same question. I left him gratefully in their care and went home.

Next morning Jack didn't turn up for work, which was quite unlike him, but he walked in looking very tired at about 1400 hours.

'Where have you been?' I asked. He muttered, 'Your bloody sailor! He said I had to take him to Netley this morning.' Netley was the nearest Ministry of Defence psychiatric hospital to us at Uxbridge. Apparently Jack had been called out, being the only R.M.N. at the hospital that night, and there was a riot going on in the officers' ward. There had been no beds on my airmen's ward for this chap so they had put him in the officers' ward with screens around his bed. His first act was to get into the bath with all his clothes on and then, on returning to the wards, he stood on his bed soaking wet and started throwing things at the officers such as urine bottles and glasses and so on. Jack arrived in the middle of this lot to find the patients huddled in the corner, glass everywhere. Then one of the junior medical officers tried to get at our sailor with a syringe to sedate him. Eventually, after a bit of a scuffle, they did this and it was arranged that Jack would escort him to Netley at 3.00 when things had calmed down a bit. They had a hairy ride in the staff car, Jack in the back with the patient, with a loaded syringe ready to plunge into him again if he played up. He said everything had been okay until they came to Epping Forest and suddenly the patient leapt forward and grabbed hold of the girl driver's hair. He thought it was a pussycat and wanted to stroke it. They nearly hit a tree. Eventually they arrived at Netley exhausted and were met by the guard commander.

'Where is the escort? Jack was asked.

'That's me,' he replied.

'Blimey!' said the staff sergeant, 'They usually send 4 blokes to cope with one like this.' The chap was a manic depressive and later I found that he had been detained at Heathrow because he had taken all his clothes off on the flight from Zurich and peed over one of the stewardesses.

Two weeks after this I was ordered to fly up to Turnhouse in Edinburgh to bring back a dying senior officer. He had cancer of the liver and wanted to be near his family in the south. We flew up in a 12-seater twin engine Percival Pembroke with seats removed to take a stretcher. When we arrived at the sick quarters at Turnhouse, the patient was actually in the charge of army staff. I went in to see him and found that he was very ill indeed and in a lot of pain. The air ambulance attendant with me noted that he had a very swollen abdomen and pointed out that if we flew too high, the gas would expand in the reduced atmosphere and could not only cause maximum pain but rupture his abdominal wound, which was only eight days old. I pointed this out to the Colonel, who didn't understand and treated me with disdain, I'm sure because I was only an NCO. However, I stuck to my guns and in the end he asked me what I wanted. I told him that we would need permission to fly down below radar coverage at about 1000 feet all the way and to increase his sedation because it was a windy day and the flight would be very bumpy, particularly over the hills, at such a low altitude. He agreed to this and the flight plan was modified. The patient was by now fast asleep and two hours later we arrived back at Uxbridge after a very bumpy flight and I saw him to his side ward and went home.

Two to three weeks later I was on night duty. When on nights, we took over three wards: the family ward, officers' ward and airmen's ward. The first night, as I was doing my rounds, I went into the side ward and found that this officer patient was still with us, much to my surprise, very ill with drips and drains and all the usual paraphernalia of the terminally ill patient. However he opened his eyes and said,

'Aren't you the chap who brought me down from Turnhouse?'

'That's right, sir,' I replied.

'Oh!' he said, 'you're the sergeant in charge of the airman's ward.' 'That's right,' I answered.

He continued, 'The one with the blue ceiling and the red doors in the toilet?'

'That's right,' I said again. At this he went back to sleep.

UXBRIDGE

Now the officers' ward was on the opposite side of the hospital to my ward and it would have needed a long walk up a set of stairs and a lift to get there, so how did he know that? No-one had told him, I was sure, but he had seen it. I had had a battle with the Ministry of Public Buildings and Works when it came to the usual time for painting the ward. The toilets had cold, red-tiled floors, white walls and white paintwork. They also faced north so they were always cold. I wanted them warmed up and we had a long discussion during which I asked for the doors to be painted red and the wall tiles to be covered with a white/pink fleck paint. It took a lot of persuading, but they did it and it looked very nice and felt a lot warmer. The main ward, being an RAF building, had pale blue walls and a white ceiling. This I persuaded them to reverse, so as to have blue ceilings and white walls, and I explained to them that most of my patients were lying in bed and a blue ceiling was better to look at, a more natural colour that white. I still did not know how the officer knew this fact, but he did, and I assumed he had had an out-of-body experience and seen it. He certainly could not have visited the ward physically. Not only was he too ill; he had no reason to do so.

On the families' ward there was a very sad case, a young 24 year-old woman who had cancer of the breast which had spread to her spine. She was married and had a young baby of some two years old. She was a very nice girl but had suffered a lot of painful surgery. In those days one of the standard treatments was to perform a bilateral adrenalectomy. This sometimes helped to slow down the spread of the disease but in her case it didn't help; she had already had both breasts removed.

We did a two-week night duty of 12 hours a night in those days, and on the first night I went into her ward about 2.30 to find her awake. She was restless and the drugs didn't seem to be helping. The weather was hot and stuffy and she was distressed. I asked her why she wasn't sleeping and she said she was thinking about her baby and husband. We talked for a little while and I held her hand while she shed a few tears. She said her feet were sore so I got a bowl of warm soapy water and towel and put her feet into the bowl and gently massaged them for about ¼ of an hour. This seemed to help so I dried them, powdered them and she went off to sleep. This then became a regular occurrence for the rest of my night duty. It would be at 2.30 each night. Then on my last night, when I had finished and tucked her up, she said, 'This is your last night, isn't it?' I said it was and she said, 'Thank you very much for what you have done for me,' and she went to sleep and never woke up. She died as I went off duty at 8.00. This was one of the many times that I realised one had such a powerful force in one's own body and mind if it was used properly. It seems that there is a transfer of energy from the strong to the weak. I know that whenever I have done anything like that since, I have always felt completely exhausted afterwards. I can't explain it but it just seems to happen.

After a week's leave, which we usually had out of our leave entitlement after night duty (and you needed it), I was back on days at the ward. The patients were mainly young men and a lot of them suffered from Hodgkin's disease or Hodgkin's Lymphoma, which caused massive swelling in the lymphatic glands in the neck, groin and sometimes internally around the liver and heart. The problem with this disease was that the swelling interfered with the blood and nervous supply to the organs and caused fresh symptoms, such as pain and jaundice and all other kinds of unpleasant conditions. The patient also became anaemic and had bleeding disorders and I saw some that literally bled to death. They needed constant haematological monitoring and often blood transfusions just to give them some quality of life. It was a most distressing disease. The ward had 24 patients and usually six of these patients would be suffering from this problem. This was out of the total RAF population of some half a million, including dependants, but you really felt that the whole world had cancer. The main treatment in these days was deep x-ray therapy, which meant that the patient had to go by ambulance every day up to the Westminster Hospital, where we had staff to irradiate them. This was exhausting to say the least and the journey did not help.

Radiation in those days, with the type of equipment that was available, was not really satisfactory. Massive burns could occur to the skin and we needed a lot of time and patience looking after skin conditions and using steroid creams. A further problem was coping with the massive nausea, vomiting and hair loss which went with the radiation.

One day the Air Vice Marshal came to do his rounds and brought with him a new drug; it was, I remember, called methalydrazine. Two capsules three times a day were to be taken specifically by those suffering with Hodgkin's. After three days the swelling on these patients began to disappear and one individual felt a lot better. By the end of the week all the swellings had gone. We and the patients were absolutely elated. A few days later we came on duty to find the swellings had all come back again and the patient, of course, absolutely in the dumps. When the AVM arrived that afternoon to examine them all, he said,

'Well, we sent him into remission for two weeks, that has never happened before and now we must make it three weeks and then a month and so on.'

This cheered us all up but the patients were all established cases and the drug needed to be given when the disease was first diagnosed. So for the first time things were on the move and I count myself to be very fortunate to have seen this really historic result. Thereafter, although things improved, it still required a lot of effort on the part of the nursing and medical staff to carry these patients along with us. Nowadays most Hodgkin's patients are readily treatable. By then some patients were being treated as outpatients, coming in only for a top up of blood or minor surgical techniques to keep them going.

Much support was given to the patient by the RAF Benevolent Fund. This could provide quite considerable help with housing and major work to existing homes to allow the patient to live his last few months at home in reasonable comfort. They would even install central heating for such patients. The RAF would take the patient and his wife off the active list and post him into the hospital so that the families became eligible for married quarters.

It made a vast difference if they could have their loved ones near them and helped considerably with the long journeys that were often needed to visit them. I recall one patient, a RAF Regiment fireman called Pete. He had Hodgkin's disease and was doing only reasonably well. He was staring out of the ward window one night looking out towards the quarters. I went up to him and said,

'What's up, Pete?'

'Oh, the wife and the kids are over there and I'm still in here.' he answered. He wasn't very happy at all.

'Would you like to go home tonight?' I asked.

'Of course I would,' he replied, 'But don't be silly, I can't do that.'

'Don't worry,' I said, 'I will clear it with the MO and take you home and settle you down and collect you in the morning.'

He was highly delighted with this. I took him home, gave him his injection and picked him up in the morning. He had a good night's sleep. I went on leave the next day and when I returned he had been discharged. It was not until some seven years later that I met his wife. She recognised me and told me that it was from that night onwards that he began to get better. Just a little bit of kindness, a little bit of help like that, was worth all the treatment in the world to him at that time.

Roger was another chap who responded quite promisingly and was well enough to go back to his unit and onto light duties. He was a tall man, over 6 feet tall; all of his hair had fallen out and he was a bit breathless but he was determined to go and the Air Vice Marshal thought it would do him good. There were one or two zealots of authority at his unit. He couldn't wear a hat because of his hair loss, so couldn't salute, and once or twice enthusiastic young officers who didn't know him tried to charge him with insubordination. Fortunately this only amused him and he went along with it until it came to the attention of the CO, who took the officer concerned apart at the seams and made him apologise to Roger. But Roger was a nice lad who bore no malice. He was married to a lovely young girl who was always welcome in the ward, and when she visited, all the patients adored her and thought what a lucky chap he was. He came back to us for one assessment and on the Saturday he asked me if he could go out to Slough on the bus to do some shopping. I cleared this with the medical officer and off he went at about 1330 hours. At 1500 hours we received a phone call from Slough police. Did we have a Roger as a patient?

'Why?' I asked.

'He has assaulted a youth in the High Street.'

'What are you going to do about it?' I asked, 'Did you know that he's very ill?'

'Yes,' they said, 'We'd better bring him back.' So twenty minutes later he arrived back on the ward. I talked to the two policemen for a minute, satisfied myself that nothing was going to happen, and then sent for Roger, who was grinning from ear to ear. Apparently he was walking down the High Street and a couple of yobos taunted him about his bald head. They were outside Halfords so he picked up one of the children's bikes out on display and wrapped it round one yobo's neck. The other one ran off. The Fire Brigade had to be called to cut the yobo free.

About a month later, Roger collapsed and was brought back to hospital extremely breathless and very, very ill. He had had a massive pulmonary effusion and for two weeks some three litres of fluid had to be drained from his lung every second day. I had never seen anything like it. The fluid was bright green. He couldn't last like this. I put him in an oxygen tent and placed him on the very, very seriously ill list and sent for his relatives. Before I went off duty a few days later, Roger was still with us and one of my nursing attendants said that he wanted to talk to me. I went over to the tent and got onto the bed beside him holding his hand,

'How much longer is this going to last,' he wheezed

'Do you think you can last like this?' I said,

'No,' he replied, 'The sooner, the better!'

I thought quickly.

'Give it a week, Roger,' I said.

'Thank you,' he said 'for everything, goodnight,' and he died at 3.00 in the morning.

TO TRAVEL HOPEFULLY

Roger was a great Scalextric fan and the next morning the adjutant phoned me and asked me to come to his office. 'There is a packet for you,' he said. In fact it was a large box full of all Roger's Scalextrics. His wife had included a little note thanking me for all we had done and asking me accept this for my two boys. I was very touched. My two lads were delighted and it was only in 1996 that I eventually disposed of the scalextrics, as they were now completely worn out. I always thought of Roger when we used them.

Sid was another Hodgkin's sufferer. He was only twenty and married, also in a terminal state like Roger, but his legs had become paralysed by Hodgkin's deposits in his spine. When lying in bed, he liked to look out of the window at the garden; he was very keen on gardening and was critical of what he saw outside. He had many gardening books and planned various gardens which he would plant when he got better. One day he asked me if he could have a window box on the ward. I wondered if that was a good idea and asked the adjutant who said, 'Not likely! There would be hell to play if it fell of and injured someone. Think again.' So I went back to see him and asked if he'd like some seed trays; he could have a garden in the ward on one of the large tables. He thought that was a marvellous idea and I told him to give me a list of what he wanted and I would go down to the local seed merchants and get the stuff for him. Sid gave me a fiver and off I went.

The seed merchant was a real professional, a bit sharp, so when I presented him with this list of seeds, he was a bit rude. 'That's no bloody good,' he said and then he started going on about chromosomes and mutations and so on and so forth. I interrupted him,

'Hang on a minute!' I said, and explained to him that Sid had got cancer and was terminally ill and needed something to pass the time and he was only twenty years old.

'Oh!' he said, 'Wait a minute, I'll get you something.' He came back a minute or so later with some geranium seeds, three big seed trays and two bags of John Innes compound.

'Give him that,' he said, 'give him that with my love. The RAF were good to me during the War when I was ill,' and he wouldn't take a penny for it.

I was delighted and Sid was pleased and so we started gardening on a table in the ward. Sid lived to see a couple of plants come to flower before he died but the other patients would not let me take Sid's plants away until they had all died off, along with many of the patients as well.

This was a period in my life when I saw a lot of death and distress but it still had its funny moments. I was young enough to take it on the chin and coped well. One day a warrant officer of the Royal Iranian Airforce was admitted. He worked at the Iranian Embassy but couldn't speak a word of English and we couldn't speak a word of Farsi. The Embassy seemed to have abandoned him and didn't come to visit him. He was a little man with a big nose. He formed an attachment to Jack and followed him around like a little dog. Everything was Jack this and Jack that, about the only word he knew, he did however know a little French, and so somehow we managed to communicate. He was being treated with cytotoxic drugs and had lost all his hair; he had a very fat face and abdomen anyway, but his legs were like sticks, and what with the steroids, he really did not look very attractive. Poor man! It was difficult keeping him in a ward and he wanted to get out into the garden. Making him understand our responsibilities to him was impossible. He started going for walks on his own, dressed only in his pyjamas, in the grounds of the hospital. One day he found a bicycle parked outside one of the offices and decided that it would be nice to ride. He started riding around the car park. Our attention was taken by something else when we suddenly realised that Abdul, as we knew him, was missing and Jack went to look for him. Five minutes later the phone rang and the guardroom told me that a little chap in pyjamas had just ridden out of the unit into the town on a bike. Was he ours? Panic stations of course. Jack got the warrant officer's bike and started off after him, eventually catching up with him as he pedalled like stink down the main street, attracting a lot of attention. He wouldn't stop. Jack finally caught up with him and cornered him. He persuaded the poor fellow to return to the hospital. It was some two hours later before he was back with us and in future all bikes were locked up and he was allowed to wear his uniform in case he absconded again. Unfortunately it did him no good. He was getting very depressed with no visits (although we made representations to the Embassy) and no letters, and he went down quickly and passed away. The Embassy still didn't want him and we had to keep his body for some three months before it could be disposed of.

We also dealt with very major surgery at Uxbridge, which required specialist attention; consultants from various UK centres of excellence would come and operate on very difficult cases. One surgeon from University College Hospital (I think it was) would operate at Uxbridge on patients with cancer of the larynx. This was a terribly mutilating operation and left the patient unable to speak after a total laryngectomy. It was technically most demanding for the surgeon and also on the nursing staff, post-operatively. The patients were left with a total tracheostomy so that they could breathe until the wound healed and they could then have speech therapy to teach them to speak again using their stomach muscles and lips to form words.

Once again it was difficult for a lot of patients to come to terms with this but the main problem was the immediate post-operative period of the first twelve hours, when massive haemorrhage could occur and the tracheostomy could fail to function properly. These patients had to be nursed in a side room surrounded with all the resuscitation equipment available, with a trained member of staff always present.

I'd been watching the surgery in the theatre as a matter of interest and when the patient was taken back to the ward, a new young Princess Mary nursing sister was put in charge of him in a side ward. After settling him down, the anaesthetist, ward sister and myself went back to the ward office for a well-earned cup of coffee, having ascertained that the patient was reasonably stable and that the sister knew what to do. We had been sitting discussing the operation when suddenly the emergency call bell rang from the side ward. It was one of those moments when we all knew that something terrible was wrong. All of us leapt to our feet, pounded into the side ward and down the corridor. As we opened the door we saw the patient, who appeared to be all right, and the PM sister, looking out of the window. Without turning round, she said a little squirrel had fallen out of the tree in the garden and was hurt. 'Would you please send for the RSPCA?' She was rapidly taken out of the ward and duly admonished. She couldn't see that she had done anything wrong anyway. The same girl, a few days later, told a patient who had intractable pain from cancer of the spine that it was God's will that we human beings should suffer pain. After that she didn't last long at Uxbridge and we packed her off somewhere else where she could do no harm!

I had by now been in the hospital since March 1964, two years, and I knew it was time I moved on. Almost to the day, I was told I was on the preliminary warning roll again for overseas. Our hospital warrant officer, another Warrant Officer Jones, had been at the medical training depot at Freckleton and knew all the people there who did the postings. I went in to see if he could find out my posting. He was a nice chap and was only too pleased to help, so he got on the phone to Freckleton.

'Hello George,' he said (whoever George was) 'I'm just doing my rota for the next six months and I wondered if you could tell me when Sergeant Snuggs is posted and where.' There was a pause, then he said,

'Right!' and turned to me saying, 'July, Cyprus.' Well that sounded good and I went home that Friday and told my wife the good news. She was pleased as it was a very good posting and the accommodation was easy to get either in quarters or in rented property. So we began to make plans but I had a nasty feeling that George at Freckleton had not said Cyprus. I was certain I heard George say MEAF (Middle East Air Force) not Cyprus. On Saturday my doubts grew and by Sunday I was convinced that it wasn't Cyprus. There were only three other units, Malta, Gibraltar and El Adem, deep in the desert, which was the only one with a small hospital and I thought, 'this is it'. A dreadful post with no accommodation for families and a long waiting list of about 10–12 months for quarters, mainly outside the unit.

On the Monday morning the orderly room phoned me. Would I go down, my posting was in. Yes I was right ... El Adem. I was furious.

'Is he in?' I said to the Corporal, pointing towards the door the other side of the office.

'Yes, he's in but he's busy you can't go in at the moment.'

'Oh can't I!', I replied and walked in to see him reading a newspaper.

'Hello,' he said and I told him

'You said Cyprus – it's not, it's El Adem! You didn't hear Cyprus, you only heard the Middle East Air Force.'

'Oh my God,' he said 'I didn't think of that. Oh dear, I'm so sorry. O crumbs!'

'So you should be!' I shouted, 'Are you going to go and tell my wife?' It was not a happy day.

So a couple of months later I was prepared once again for another unaccompanied tour of some 10 months. This time to a dirty, dusty, flyblown desert place in Libya. I knew a bit about El Adem by this time, having been through it twice, so I knew it wouldn't be any good taking my car out there in those conditions. It broke my heart again to have to sell it and as everybody knew I was going, offers were few and far between. I eventually got £125 for it and had to sell it on a monthly standing order into my account at £15 a month. So that was the car.

Each posting gets more difficult but this time, with a lot of quarters available, my wife was told that she would be able to stay in quarters at Uxbridge until she joined me in possibly nine months' time. Just before I left, I went down to the electricity office, told them I would be leaving and asked them to cut the supply when my wife phoned to say, and send me the bill via the Sergeants' Mess at El Adem. But they couldn't do that and informed me that I would have to pay before I went. I said that wouldn't be possible as my wife was dealing with the money.

UXBRIDGE

'Sorry,' they said 'But you can't go overseas until you pay, then the power is cut off.' I left them my address and advised them to communicate their views to the Staff of the Minister of Defence, Whitehall, London and see if he would help. They didn't see the point so I just laughed and walked out. So once again in July I was on my way, saying goodbye to my wife and family, not knowing when I would see them again. In this way one of the most interesting postings in my life, or so I thought, came to an end . . . but life could only get easier. I should have known better, surely!

CHAPTER SEVEN

Middle East

Once again I presented myself to RAF Lyneham for disposal and within an hour I was on an old Comet 2 transport, bound for El Adem via Benina, the airport for Benghazi where we refuelled for the short hop to our destination. I arrived at 7 p.m. and booked into the mess, where I was allocated a room in an old Nissen hut with no lights . . . they had all fused. There was just a bed and bedside table. This was just until I could get a better room in the mess itself, I was told.

It was 8 p.m. now and pitch dark. Nobody had met me from station sick quarters; nobody knew I was coming, I subsequently discovered, and I sat on the bed in the complete darkness and the heat. The fan didn't work and it felt like the end of the world. It was July, the hottest time of the year, and the flies wouldn't leave me alone. However, picking myself up with the help of a small hand torch, I unpacked, settled down and fell asleep exhausted. Flying always tires me out. It's not that I don't like flying but it is usually so complicated and tiring and the food often so abysmal.

I awoke the next morning, got into my khaki drill and walked across to the mess for breakfast. It was hot even at 0700 hours. What a prospect! Sand, rock, desert. No trees or distinguishing features. I walked into the mess and sat down at one of the tables and the waiter brought me a plate of greasy bacon and tomatoes. At that moment a warrant officer came into the dining room.

'Gentlemen,' he announced, everyone stopped eating and looked up, 'Today for the first time since I have been here in 4 weeks I have passed a formed stool!' A great cheer from the other mess members went up to greet this announcement. 'Oh dear!' I thought, 'It's going to be like that!' and within 24 hours I had the trots.

MIDDLE EAST

Sick quarters was a typical RAF set-up, almost identical to Gan and most other stations sick quarters in tropical places. The SMO was a Wing Commander Rogers. He had two junior medical officers, both flight lieutenants, who greeted me warmly and admitted straight away that they had no idea why I was posted in because they already had three PM sisters in post and a couple of civilians who were SRNs, and there was not a lot of work to do anyway. I thought the whole idea of posting me in was a bit daft. The senior SMO thought he should contact Cyprus headquarters and request a transfer for me to Akrotiri Hospital in Cyprus. In the meantime, as he was going on leave for a month, it would have to wait until he came back and then he would talk to me about it again. The Senior NCO was a flight sergeant, Jones again; they were all Jones's in the RAF medical branch. It was suggested that I just found something useful to do for the next month. There's nothing quite so demoralising as a situation like this, so I went to meet the three PMs, all nice girls, all midwives – that was about the only type of work needed on a unit like this, apart from attending to the usual gut upsets or simple conditions requiring the minimum of care.

The rest of the week was usually GP work, so realising I was surplus to requirements, I thought I must have been posted here by somebody who had a grudge against me for my six years with Air Commodore Soper. So I had three days of messing about. There was nothing to do after duty but play cards and read in the mess; nowhere to walk to and not really enough men on the unit even to be able to choose compatible companions. In fact these bases were slowly running down and El Adem was really only a refuelling base with few other commitments; most people were on shifts to keep the place going. I went in to see the senior of the two medical officers, who listened to what I had to say and was sympathetic. He suggested that I would probably be better off down on the coast at the small RAF garrison at Tobruk, where at least there were the married quarters in the town, and a bigger population of families would give me something to do. I jumped at the chance and that afternoon I arrived in the mess at the garrison of Tobruk, some 30 miles across the desert down on the coast.

In comparison to El Adem, Tobruk was almost civilised. The town itself was a typical Arab town. Many Arab entrepreneurs had built blocks of flats, which were rented out to the airmen and their families. El Adem had a number of quarters but it was quite insufficient for even half the number of staff that were there then, so the majority of the 300 men of El Adem and their families lived in Tobruk. The old army garrison was used by the RAF as a base and contained all the stores, NAAFI, school, sick quarters etc.; all the requirements for a modern RAF unit. It was all housed in old Italian buildings which were pre-war and always difficult to maintain and had scruffiness built into them.

The CO of the garrison was an RAF Squadron Leader who was quite pleasant and welcomed me, as did the chief clerk. The latter, much to the surprise of the local Arabs, was working and living amongst us, although he was West Indian and as black as the ace of spades. Jasper was, after all, a warrant officer but he was a very nice chap. We also had in residence, at any one time, a couple of army companies, different regiments who were training in desert warfare and also a tank squadron or two. These also reminded the Libyans that we were a force to be reckoned with in the event of a difficult diplomatic situation. The relations however were good and it was 1966, just two years before Colonel Gadaffi took over and the King and his court often lived in the palace in the town behind the mosque. This RAF unit gave him some security.

My role was to be in charge of the small station sick quarters, which had two consulting rooms, a living room and duty room, a dental surgery, treatment room and the usual offices. The SMO or the junior medical officer visited daily from 8.00 until 12 and once a week an antenatal clinic was held by the Princess Mary's nursing sister also attending. We had about 300 families of Mum, Dad and 2 and 5/8 children and about 100 soldiers to keep an eye on.

I booked into the mess and then went to have a look at my new domain but the door of the station sick quarters was shut

Tobruk, Libya. Station sick quarters.

and locked. I rang the bell but nobody came. On the door was a notice that said, 'Duty nursing attendant in the Churchill Club'. This was a good start, I thought. If some mother with an unconscious child in her arm turned up, where/what was the Churchill Club? I went to find the mess steward to show me around.

The Churchill Club was the NAAFI and there I found the nursing attendant having a drink. He was a corporal and not at all pleased to have me there. We returned to the station sick quarters and went into the office. I looked over the documentation, the stores, arrangements for work. Apparently we did not have a very good sick parade as the patients preferred to go to the chemist locally and get their own treatment. Some, I eventually found, were actually getting controlled drugs for the relief of pain and any antibiotic they wanted locally.

The families did not have a lot of faith in the RAF medical system and on investigation, I found there was no visiting by the MO in the town. Each morning anyone who phoned up for a visit was simply collected by ambulance and brought up to sick quarters to see the MO. The soldiers would also appear sick, wearing full combat gear and bringing their rifles and other accoutrements with them into sick quarters. This did not go down too well with the female patients, so many women did not attend and there were even more reasons to keep them away, I discovered. So a lot of bridge-building was required and confidence in the system needed to be restored. In fact the system itself needed to be rebuilt. The sick quarters were a mess; no seats in the waiting room, bare walls, the duty bunk in the living area an absolute tip. The duty medics from the army companies, usually the dimmest members, so far as I could see, were also used by the SSQ while they were in residence, and I discovered that they would hand out medicines without any prescription by the MO, with the result that there had been quite a number of cases of drug poisoning already. Having looked at this lot, I asked to see the other staff. It consisted of one junior nursing attendant and a driver. The driver apparently was a good lad and he was most helpful. Even he didn't like what he saw. So at least I had an ally. After surveying this lot, I looked around and announced that in future there would be 24-hour cover at station sick quarters. One nursing attendant on duty for the full 24 hours and one off, and I would be on call at all times. If forays to the NAAFI were necessary, I was to be informed. Also, anyone requiring emergency treatment would be seen by me first of all and only if I felt it necessary or if the patient wanted it, would they then be sent to El Adem if it was after duty hours. This was a long way to go in an ambulance for simple things. I also announced that I would in future work in the treatment room and do all the dispensing and the treatments and leave the nursing attendants to do the administration, which I must admit wasn't in good order.

So again I settled in to the mess. This was pleasant, bright and airy and comfortable, so much nicer than the Nissen hut, and now I was able to run things my way. The garrison itself, although it was dirty and dusty, was a reasonably attractive area and had plenty of trees, and so had quite a lot of shade. At dinner that night a number of senior NCOs I had met before were in the mess. So this was rather pleasant. They were mainly marine craft section people and I had worked with them when I was in Gan, so I was among friends again.

I was called the first night at 11 p.m. A one year old child was in the treatment room unconscious with the nursing attendant. When I arrived, he was trying to sit the child up, much to the consternation of its parents. It was obvious he didn't know what to do. I took one look and laid the boy down in the recovery position and had another look. He had a maximum dilated right pupil and was very hot, with a temperature of 101. I sponged him down and got the ambulance out and we arrived at sick quarters half an hour later, from where he was eventually transferred by air the next day to Cyprus. This was a good start. I realised how very vulnerable these families were without medical help and I was determined to improve what was basically a disaster of a service.

The next morning the medical officer arrived for his clinic, which comprised about twenty people, and after this various people crept in for free medicines, which had been handed out to friends etc. by the staff. This was going to stop and I told both nursing attendants I would charge anybody who gave out medicines without the MO's prescription properly filled in.

We also had a SSAFA sister, Miss Flight, who was a health visitor. She handled the young children, the post-natal and paediatric work, and was a great help – we got on very well together. I could confide in her professionally as she was a very experienced nurse and acted as a good sounding board in difficult cases. Unfortunately she did not do calls, so the evenings and the nights were very much my responsibility.

By this time I was beginning to be known and other Department Heads were co-operating well. I had been in post about a week when I was called out at midnight to see a six-month old baby who had breathing difficulties and was a known asthmatic. We had had a relatively cold spell, as sometimes happens in September in the desert, and when I got to the house I could hear her respiratory distress from the door. None of the drugs had worked and when I got into their living room I saw why; the only source of heating they had was a paraffin stove and this was on full with a yellow flame. I quickly turned it out, wrapped her up well and took her into the next room, which was much cooler with no heater. I then called the electrician to get an electric fire on loan until the next day, when we could sort it all out. This solved the problem and the parents were most grateful. Fortunately the boss of stores had needed my help the day before, so 'you scratch my back and I scratch yours' worked well and it continued to do so throughout my two years in post.

The alarms and excursions continued for the next six weeks and then the SMO returned. I showed him what I had been doing and the improvements I had introduced and he was most grateful. All the MOs had feared anything going wrong in Tobruk, where they could spend so little time because of the commitment to the airfield and the maternity unit, so to have some of the load lifted was much appreciated. I asked the SMO about the transfer to Cyprus and he asked me if I would wait until after the Command Medical Secretarial Officer's and the Command Senior Matron's Inspection in two weeks time ... 'They want to talk to you,' he said.

Two weeks later the Command Medical Officer arrived with the SMO and had a look around. He took me to the office and straight away said,

'You want to go to Cyprus.'

'That's right, sir,' I replied.

'The SMO has told me that you are head and shoulders above the rest here and you are doing a good job,' he continued.

'Anybody could do this,' I answered equally bluntly.

'But' he countered, 'They don't! ... Don't be a bloody fool. If you go to Cyprus you will be a small fish in a big pond and will get only average assessments. Stay here and you will do all right. I can almost guarantee it, if you keep your nose clean.'

'It's the quarters that are a problem,' I said.

'I know,' he said, 'You have only been back from Gan for a year, bear with me. Anyway, Miss Cagill the matron wants to see you,' and with that he walked out.

MIDDLE EAST

Miss Cagill then came in. I had known her for some time at Halton when I was in theatre and we got on very well. We shook hands and she then referred to the conversation I had had with the Wing Commander. She told me that a lot of others were worried about the state of staffing in sick quarters. One day there would be a tragedy and heads would roll. Would I stay please?

'What about the family?' I asked.

'I'll see about that if you will stay,' she offered. It was strange to be asked. Well what else could I do? I had to admit it, it was interesting and I was virtually my own boss.

So I soldiered on but now with a greater sense of purpose, accepting the responsibility. Now I started making a lot of improvements to the Department to make it a pleasanter place in which to care for the sick. I was visiting patients at home and cajoled the MOs to do the same when necessary. The numbers on sick parade were rising and the army no longer brought their weapons in. Although it was tiring and I was the only one, it was very pleasant work.

About a week after this, the MO phoned me and asked me if I would join him on a jolly. We were to go out deep into the desert to cover a parachute drop that was coming in from Cyprus. This would be a joint exercise with the Desert Rescue Group, the Libyan Army Desert Rescue and Transport Command. We flew out in a small Percival Pembroke 12-seater, landed at Benina, refuelled and then flew on. We were 10 in number, various specialists, all officers except for myself, and the aircraft was heavily loaded. We continued on the last part of the journey over the Gulf of Sirte, then turned hard to port into the desert. At that point we encountered a very strong head wind. I realised something was wrong because we seemed not to be moving. Some 5000 feet below was an ancient Roman archway over the road to Tripoli and Benghazi and I had been looking at it from the same position for a couple of minutes or so. The captain of the aircraft, a warrant officer, turned round and shouted to one of the passengers to crawl very slowly to the rear of the aircraft on hands and knees and pull a couple of heavy radio batteries along the floor towards the nose of the aircraft. As the man slowly moved back we felt the aircraft tip and then, as he reached the boxes and began to drag them, the nose of the aircraft dropped and we began to move forwards again. Quite a hairy moment and one which very experienced flyers in older aircraft were used to, but I was only experienced in flying in heavy and fast jet aircraft and hadn't realised what real flying was like. As we gathered speed again and the coast disappeared beneath us, we started over the real desert, rock, mountains, sand dunes and little else – it looked utterly harsh and uninviting.

After a couple of hours we descended to a rather bumpy landing on an old airstrip which had been bulldozed flat by an oil company and sprayed with crude oil to give it a hard surface. It was a very short runway, just long enough for us to get down. To understand the real meaning of silence you need to leave a propeller-driven aircraft and stand in the desert for a moment. As we got out of the aircraft, I turned to the MO I was with and said,

'Well, listen to that.'

'What?' he asked.

'Yes, precisely!' I responded.

The Western Desert is supposed to be one of the least inhabited places on earth but, as often happens, almost immediately we were being observed by an Arab herdsman, very scruffy, with legs scarred with desert sores, in charge of a few scrawny camels. We had noted them from the air before landing, standing under an escarpment about a quarter of a mile from the airstrip. On top of the escarpment was a fort looking like a Beau Geste creation and the camels and herdsman had all moved towards the strip as we came in for landing, doubtless hoping for some largesse.

We unloaded the tents, sleeping bags and all the paraphernalia of a camp site from the aircraft while the skipper tried to get in touch by radio with the Desert Rescue people coming out from El Adem and the Libyans from Tripoli. The tents were pitched and our sleeping bags laid out under the aircraft and a meal of beans, sausage and mashed potato was prepared and eaten. Eventually, at about 10 p.m. that night, the other two groups arrived with three

Land Rovers, and after quite a rowdy party, we all settled down for the night to await the arrival of the parachute drop the next morning.

Lying on our backs under the aircraft in the desert was a strange experience. There was no moon but the stars were brilliant, and with no water vapour in the air, so that one felt one could almost touch them. They seemed to be like punched-out holes of brilliant light in the black sky. It was absolutely still apart from the occasional sound of a stone being moved by some desert creature. Then slowly a gentle wind began to blow from the south from the mountains we had seen in the distance and, as the sand began to move very, very slightly, one could hear a gentle whine as the grains of sand brushed against each other. It was so quiet and peaceful that I began to doze off.

An hour after midnight my colleague and I sat up with a jolt. A sudden roar broke out in a rush of sound and was gone. I hit my head on the undercarriage of the aircraft and cursed. 'What was that?' My colleague delivered the memorable lines:

'Probably a wild animal and probably more frightened of us than we are of it.'

'Oh yes!' thought I, 'I hope the animal knows that!' Next morning when we got up, no more than 10 yards from us in the sand, were the tracks of a large animal. The CO reckoned it was a mountain lion, which was common in these parts, but it would not have attacked us as the smell of oil from the plane would have put it off. He said!!

After breakfast of beans, sausage and potatoes again (potatoes fried this time however!) the skipper contacted Cyprus, to be told that there was a 24-hour delay in the parachute jump due to the weather in Cyprus, so it was up to us to find something to do. About 10 a.m., after cleaning up the camp, the crockery was all rubbed over with sand, which cleaned it beautifully – we could not waste water on washing up – and we set off in the Land Rover to follow the tracks of the mountain lion. We followed them down the escarpment for about a mile and at the bottom was a small swamp surrounded by hundreds of camel bones. It was a

TO TRAVEL HOPEFULLY

sort of camel graveyard and the lions obviously came down at night to feed off the carcasses.

On the way back, we found the Beau Geste castle at the top of the escarpment. It was a relic of the Italian occupation of Libya and was still surrounded by barbed wire. We struggled up the escarpment and over the wire and came to the big metal gates at the back. Written on them in chalk was a large sign which said, much to our amusement, that Kilroy was not here. We poked around for a little while, finding little of interest but marvelling at the fortitude of the troops that had lived here in these conditions, and then went back to the Land Rovers. It was getting hot and the flies were beginning to become a nuisance; they crept into your eyes, your ears, up your nose – they were most unpleasant but a typical feature of desert life. We settled down in what little shade there was to while away the time.

After tea at about 6 p.m., the MO said to me that he thought he'd seen a water hole some distance from the camp.

'Let's go and get a wash!' he said. Yes, we found the hole in a nearby wadi, with a goatskin bag and a rope beside it. Looking down we could see water about 20 feet below.

'Okay,' he said, 'You first!' He let down the rope and pulled up a bag brimming with water and dumped it over me. It was icy cold. I don't really expect it was more than 70° but the air temperature was over 100° and it really took my breath away. It was superb! As I was about to do the same to him, there was a click click behind us and we turned around to see an Arab standing there pointing a rifle at us.

'Yes sir, three bags full sir,' we said and retreated in good order. At least I had had my bath.

Just before it got dark, I wandered off up to the top of one of the rocky outcrops to see the camp from above. I struggled to the summit to find three Bedouin sitting there with rifles looking down on us and again I retreated in good order. An uninhabited area it may have been, but it was very eerie to feel that wherever we were, we were under surveillance the whole time. However there are some things to learn in every situation and I realised

MIDDLE EAST

then, very clearly, that in the desert water meant life, no water meant death. It was as simple as that and there were no shades of grey. I was not surprised then that that Arab pointed a rifle at us.

After a quiet night, the next morning was fine and clear and the drop was due at 10.30 a.m. The aircraft, a Hastings, arrived in time and two men jumped out and landed within walking distance of us. Both were okay so we packed up to go. Unfortunately we now had two extra passengers but only room for one; one chap volunteered to go back in the Land Rover to El Adem, leaving no seats, but a stretcher was available. 'Oh!' they said, 'Who is going to go on that?' Surprise, surprise! Being the only NCO, I 'volunteered'. The skipper said: 'It's got no harness so hang on like stink. It's going to be a bumpy takeoff.' The runway was uphill and the weather was hot with no wind, so the pilot took the plane to the very end and ran up the engines as far as he could. We hurtled down the bumpy track, hit the ridge at the end and soared up into the sky. When I recovered from this, I settled down and found flying on a stretcher in an aircraft was the way to travel.

We arrived back at Benina to refuel and the Wing Commander in charge asked me if I was okay on the stretcher.

'Yes, most comfortable,' I replied.

'Okay, you nip off and I will get on.'

'No way!' I said. 'You wouldn't do it in the first place, this is my pitch!' So I went to sleep for the rest of the trip home. He wouldn't talk to me after that. I'd had a nice little holiday and I had taken some interesting slides of our jaunt, one of which won me first prize in a photography competition later.

By now I was really settling into the mess and the job and beginning to enjoy myself. I had been told that my wife and family would be out by October 12th, so was looking forward to this immensely. This was quite remarkable. The matron had been as good as her word and had pulled strings.

The work at station sick quarters continued. I was responsible for some of the hygiene aspects of life on the unit. One of our problems was the water supply, which was intermittent. The water came from deep wells at Derna, some 150 miles away, by pipe line and the supply was dependent upon the good will of the Libyans and also the demands of other Arab towns on the route of the pipeline. It ran over-ground and was pumped up into a water tower just inside the garrison perimeter. It then flowed into a holding tank at the base of the tower, where it was supposed to be chlorinated. It was the responsibility of the station sick quarters to see that the water was sufficiently treated and safe to use. An automatic chlorinator was fitted into the holding tank in which we put water sterilising powder once a week – or were supposed to – unfortunately the chlorinator was broken and had been for some six months. Although I repeatedly requested a replacement, it was always 'it has been ordered', so each day we had to throw some water sterilising powder in the tank and test it by hand. I got fed up with this and just threw in a handful a day anyway. I used the rule of thumb method so when I went into the mess and the mess members were all red-eyed and moaning, 'What the hell are you doing to the water?', I knew there was enough WSP in it for the time being. One day, climbing up to the top of the tank, I found half a dozen dead pigeons floating in the super-chlorinated water. The health of the unit was quite good – we never really had any gut upsets so we must have been doing something right.

It was now about a month before my wife and family arrived and I realised I had been foolish not to have brought my car out with me. Very few people had cars but I needed transport to get around. The service mini and ambulance were okay but you couldn't use these for private work and the RAF bus service was an hourly one to the beach. It would pick up in the town and the garrison and return to El Adem.

There were a lot of places to go. The war had ended just 20 years previously and a lot of the debris was left over, some of it extremely interesting. The Siege of Tobruk was famous and has since been written up by numerous writers, but in 1968 not much had been recorded and I wanted to go and find out more. The place was living history. It had been fought over during the centuries: the north African coastal areas had been the granary of

Tobruk town from the top of our block of flats.

the Roman Empire until the Arab arrived with his goats and herds and destroyed it all. The remains of Roman and Greek civilisation were just about everywhere, just under the surface in many places, and I was interested and wanted to discover about it all. Most of the people posted to North Africa wanted to get home as quickly as possible because of the heat and the dust, but now I was stuck for the full two-year tour so I wanted to take advantage of it and really explore.

One of our medical officers was posted home in October and asked me one day if I knew anybody who wanted to buy his 1 year-old Ford Cortina. He wanted £600 for it but I told him it was too much, as a new one was only £660 at that time. However he said that he couldn't afford to take any less. The Royal Navy transport was coming through from the Far East and was taking vehicles on board and he either had to sell the car or book a passage on it within the next two weeks. I told him that I'd put a notice in the mess for him but thought it too expensive. After a fortnight there was no response and he had missed the deadline or had forgotten about the ship. I suggested that he drove it home but he had a Jaguar and a Triumph at home and didn't need it. 'But I do!' I thought and, after seeing the car, was determined to get it. I advised him to put the price down to £500 and he still had no offers, so I suggested £400. He was most unhappy with this but I left it with him for a couple of days and then pressed him on it and at last he agreed. If anybody would buy it for £400, he would sell. I pulled out my cheque book and bought it there and then.

'You bastard!' he said, 'You were waiting for that, weren't you?' So I got a very good car for £400 sterling with 2000 miles on the clock, just in time for arrival of the family.

On the day before commencement of leave (we were entitled to two weeks' leave when the family arrived, to enable us all to settle in), I took over a flat. It was a very large and airy place on the ground floor in a block of flats in the town, not far from the King's Palace. It was the first inside the door and was well furnished and clean.

I went out and stocked the fridge with food. We had a reasonable NAAFI and could get a limited amount of most things but meat was all frozen and only of average quality, though it was adequate. The main problem in the town was the lack of a continuous supply of water or electricity. There were always power cuts, so we didn't keep too much in the fridge and we lived mainly on canned foods. The water only came in every few days.

The next day, Tuesday, my wife and the children were arriving at 2 p.m. at El Adem so I went to the NAAFI and bought a 'welcome to Libya' present, a complete Kenwood food processor with all the fittings. I was quite proud of myself and, walking out with this expensive gift on my arm, promptly fell down the steps of the NAAFI and sustained a bad injury to my ankle for my pains. As I lay writing in agony on the ground, one of the service policemen came along, got the ambulance and helped me to it. I hobbled into the station sick quarters to be met by the SMO.

'I'm busy,' he said. 'Where the hell have you been?'

'Don't worry about that! What about my ankle?' I replied.

MIDDLE EAST

'I will look at that later. There is a patient to see.' I collapsed to the floor in pain, so one of the nursing attendants bandaged it up and got me to the car, with the Kenwood, and I drove home. Fortunately I could drive okay as the injury was to my left foot, which was only needed for the clutch. I rested for the remainder of the day with my foot up and presented myself the next day at the transit mess to await the arrival of the aircraft from Malta. Unfortunately it was delayed for two hours on that island so I had to hang around. I went down to the station sick quarters and got the radiographer to x-ray my ankle just for something to do and to my surprise I found a chip fracture of the tibia.

'Give me those plates,' I said and went into the SMO's office.

'Hello!' he said, 'I thought you were on leave.' I told him about the delay to the aircraft and then I asked, 'Have you paid your medical defence fees this year?'

'Yes, why?' he replied. I said my ankle was fractured.

'What?' he said, looking worried as he grabbed the x-ray from me. He examined it and laughed and said 'it's only a chip fracture'. 'I know,' I said, 'but that shook you.' Fortunately he was one of the sort of senior officers you could talk to like that.

So I met the family at 4.00, my wife and children having had their first plane journey, and after a happy reunion we drove home in my new car. But as we crossed the desert, I could see my wife's face dropping as she saw the view of sand and rocks. Luckily it eased off as we arrived in the town, now the sun had gone down and she saw the lights of the town and arrived at our flat.

We settled in reasonably well, apart from my daughter almost having hysterics when the first thing she did was to stand on a monster cockroach with her bare feet, but this was an occupational hazard in North Africa. My wife accepted that the flat was the best we could get in the circumstances and, by buying a few bits and pieces and pictures, within a week or so it was home.

I had to leave the car outside my flat but I had been warned that if I did this the Arabs would take everything off it: the wheels, the windscreen washers and wipers and anything that could be removed. Fortunately I had made the acquaintance of the local Chief of the Traffic Police and I had patched up an injury to one of his chaps a few days previously, so I let him know about my car and he let it be known that no-one in the town was to touch the car and they never did.

Lieutenant Ali was a good chap, but more about him later. Our main domestic need was to get a reasonable water supply and about every four to five days the water came in through the pipeline from Derna to the town and filled the holding tank. This had then to be pumped up to the roof tank but before we could use any water in the house, it needed boiling and chemically sterilising, such were the dangers to health in this Third World town. Of course if no water did arrive, and we had to order water from El Adem, it came via tanker from deep wells in the desert and was pumped into our own tank. This was clean and fresh but we still boiled it.

Although the flat had a basic European type of plumbing, the drainage outside was a septic tank. These often overflowed as they were rarely emptied, the local authority taking the view that once a septic tank had been fitted, that was that. Of course, ours being the downstairs flat, we had all the overflow in our yard when the tanks filled up, but we were comfortable in our flat even though it was noisy.

No windows were fitted in the frames, only fly mesh and shutters for cold weather, so the noise of the streets, donkeys braying, pi dogs roaming round in packs barking at all hours of day and night, the locals shouting – all this kept us awake until we got used to it all. None of the locals could drive a car without using a horn.

The town and garrison gave us some entertainment. There was a cinema on the base, some shops in the town, a Salvation Army bookshop and tea-room which we called the Sally Bash, and, of course, the beach. All the messes had their own beach and our own sergeants' mess beach had a small cafeteria which sold fizzy drinks called gazoosas, of various colours and dubious flavours.

Tobruk garrison from the main gate.

Most of the children preferred the white gazoosas but any fizzy drink, Coke, Pepsi etc., came under this generic heading.

These were made locally and, by and large, the quality was acceptable. But on two occasions families complained to me of finding cockroaches and other strange oddities in a bottle, so one was always a little wary and it was easier to make your own or take a flask of tea or coffee on an outing.

The beach was naturally very popular, with clean sand, but the sea was not always so clean; the Arabs using it as a dump for rubbish and toilet purposes. I remember swimming one day about 20 yards from shore and colliding with a couple of dead sheep. All the children learnt to swim in the warm sea and it really was one of the plus points in a generally low-key environment.

The other source of comfort was the church, which was built just over the way from the Royal Palace Square and was usually well attended for the Sunday services. The popularity of the church naturally depended upon the personality of the priest in charge or the church minister who was posted in. We had two very good padres who were a great asset to us. The church club was active, the Boy Scouts were associated with it and both my boys joined and derived lots of fun from this organization. The local Libyans also had a scout troop but they preferred marching and parading as a semi-military group, so we had little to do with them. One of my tasks was to act as an examiner for the scouts' first aid course and I also helped with the exams at the school in human biology.

Our next-door neighbours were an Egyptian teacher and his wife who totally ignored us. This was in the days of Colonel Nasser and anti-British sentiment was rife in Egypt, but we were tolerated in Libya. On the other side was a poor Libyan family with numerous children who would stand and look through the mesh window while we were gathered round the table for a meal. This was annoying so we had to eat with the shutters down and the light on for many meals.

The Arab children were always decidedly scruffy and dirty, and we were advised by our own authorities to leave well alone or they would become a general nuisance. One day an RAF neighbour of ours asked me if I would look at the hand of a four year-old boy who lived next door to her. I reluctantly agreed and after a bit of pressure he came round to the flat with his equally scruffy sister. I had a nasty feeling that this would all go pearshaped. But I was pressured into it and found that the child had a horseshoe abscess on his hand, which was pointing between his thumb and forefinger. I let the pus out, which relieved him straight away, and gave him a bottle of penicillin. It cleared up almost at once but three days later he was at the door again, this time covered with the most terrible impetigo I had ever seen. I wasn't expecting this but of course no more antibiotics! Let their own bodies sort it out. I learned my lesson there.

There was another unpleasant trick played on the Europeans by the local Arab children. The doorbell would ring and when you answered it, there would be four six year-olds standing there holding young pi dog puppies. These little dogs, like all young dogs, were very appealing with brown fur and big brown eyes. 'Ten piastres!' they would chant, 'You buy?' and if you said no, they would threaten to strangle the dog, demanding fifteen piastres until you gave way. If not, the dog would die there and then. You had to be very strong to resist and shut the door because if you paid them and kept the dog, they did it again and again all round the quarters. If, however, the family took the dog in, it would make a delightful pet initially until about four months old, by which time it would have grown to the size of a small labrador and would then nip the children as the dingo came out in it. They were really wild dogs and could never have been domesticated or got rid of. If they were pushed out of the house after this, the other wild packs of pi dogs would attack them, drive them off and injure them badly.

Life was pretty basic but we soon got used to the dust, the noise and the heat and made the most of it. Friends were essential and, with me being on call 24 hours a day seven days a week, my wife found that she was often alone for long hours. But the work was there and all those families needed a lot of help. Many a young woman with a child, or pregnant and away from Mum for the first time in her life, in a dirty little Arab town with husband on shift duty 24 hours at a time, would find herself extremely vulnerable. Coping with the cockroaches, scorpions and flies alone proved extremely difficult to someone brought up gently in the West.

At the station's sick quarters I had had a change of staff. The new corporal was Welsh and very helpful. He was an ex-third year student nurse who had been thrown off a course for being drunk on duty, and so he had some understanding of the problems we found. I also had a new nursing attendant called Livings, who was proving to be a continual pain in the neck, and I had to train them both my way. The new SMO had been posted in too and although different from W/Cdr Rogers, whom he replaced, was easy to work with. He came down to do a clinic every other day from 9 to 12 and the junior medical officer did the other three days, leaving me with the rest of the week.

The even tenor of our days was often upset by the unexpected, however. One day the flight sergeant in charge of the SSQ, who lived in Tobruk, phoned and asked me to give his landlord a tube of Savlon for his niece, who had burnt herself. He would call at my flat that evening on the way home if that was ok. The man arrived with an armed guard in a big Mercedes car and as I handed him the Savlon cream, he asked me if I would come and see his niece, so I agreed and went to fetch my uniform and hat.

'No, not tonight,' he said, 'I'm rather busy.' He arranged to come round the next night and pick me up. The next evening the big Merc arrived with the guard and I was taken to a huge villa on the outskirts of Tobruk. We walked through a number of opulent rooms until we came to the women's quarters, where his wife took me over and ushered me into a small room where a young girl aged about 14 was lying in bed. The upper part of her body was swathed in bandages. She had been treated somewhere!

Through an interpreter I asked what was going on and he said that she had been in the Arab hospital and wasn't doing very well, and as I had agreed to see her, they had discharged her against advice. I should have walked out straight away but when they told me what had happened, I was quite appalled. She had failed her exams at school and so had poured petrol over herself and set herself alight. Out of compassion I agreed to see what I could do, being amply experienced in burns. I took her up to station sick quarters to examine her in an aseptic atmosphere. She had full thickness burns on her neck and chest, her nipples were burnt away and her hands were badly affected. The burns were infected and she was in great pain and not sleeping or eating. I had to go back to square one and get her antibiotics and treat her in saline baths, daily dressing her burns with saline dressings. Her diet was changed to include a lot of protein and carbohydrate and after a week she became very much improved. It was getting warm again and, as the winter had passed, the water shortage was developing. It was becoming a problem and I was dubious about continuing the baths, but she began to heal really well and in a fortnight would be ready for skin grafting. The uncle enquired about his niece and I told him she would need plastic surgery, asking if he could get her to Egypt, where I understood there was a good plastic surgery department at Alexandria City Hospital, run by the East Germans. He agreed to do this but had to go to Benghazi to get permission from the Ministry of Health to get her a passport. So off he went, saying he would be back in a couple of days. Three weeks went by and I was getting desperate. I was by now having to treat her by cutting away a lot of the granulation tissue, which was overgrowing the wounds. Also there was scar tissue forming and it was beginning to tighten up, with subsequent contractures, which would make movement impossible if proper skin grafting, splinting and physio were not started rapidly.

One day I went to see the family and they told me the uncle would be back the next day. And so the night before she was to leave, I dressed her burns in big saline packs, sent her home and breathed a sigh of relief that I wouldn't see her any more. Two weeks later the guard was knocking on my door again asking me to come and see the boss's niece.

'Certainly,' I said. 'Was she back and okay?'

'No,' he replied. 'The uncle never came back from Benghazi. He stayed and had a holiday. She is very ill.'

I really don't know, after all these years, how I did what I did and why I did it but I said no. I suddenly realised the enormity of what I had done and shut the door. I should never have agreed to treat her in the first place because, quite frankly, all I did was to extend her death not her life. For an Arab girl like that to attempt suicide was completely out of character. Insh'allah! A general statement with hands held up, or as God wills, covered everything. Also the girl was now unmarriageable, no children would ever be born, she would be useless, in Arab terms, as a woman. It was a salutary lesson again that a lot of do-gooders would be advised to learn when they interfere in others' cultural affairs with no knowledge of the outcome of the situation. The road to hell is indeed paved with good intentions.

I did have one happy result some weeks later. Lieutenant Ali, the traffic policeman, asked me to look at his wife's hands. She had a severe attack of acute dermatitis in both hands and the local hospital had failed to help her. I treated her with an antibiotic steroid cream and stopped her using a particular type of detergent to which she appeared to be allergic. The hands cleared up completely and she was so delighted. Lieutenant Ali asked me if I would see the child of his friend Lieutenant Said, who was in the army. His new baby boy was not thriving and I agreed to see him and found the child to have a fungal infection of the lung. His main problem was hunger. He was failing to thrive and at the age of six months, was only twice his normal birth weight. I quizzed the mother through an interpreter about breastfeeding and she said her breasts were too small to feed the baby. On examining her, I found she was not only extremely anaemic and not producing any milk, but as I also suspected, she had hookworm. So I taught her how to use the bottle to feed the baby with baby milk, getting the food and gear from the NAAFI, and I also treated the hookworm for her, giving her strict instructions not to attempt to breastfeed the child. They both got better. The child thrived and the mother was much improved. The parents were, of course, delighted as this was their first son, very important to an Arab, and said that in future their child would be an English child! He was already called Idris after the King, so obviously was going to be an advantaged child.

Some little time later one of our Arab auxiliaries asked me to see his baby, which had a similar problem. This time the mother had bilateral breast abscesses and she was feeding the baby pure pus. I fixed them up with bottle feeding material and gave the mother antibiotics, but she wouldn't co-operate and the baby died a week later. All in the will of Allah, said the baby's father.

It was after this rather sad episode that I fell foul of the Army. The Royal Irish Rangers were posted in and the medic, Lance Corporal Bill McCloughlin, came to work at the sick quarters. He was over 50 and had been up and down the promotion ladder numerous times in his 30 years, from staff sergeant right back down to private again for various reasons – usually it was the booze, I believe. He was a cheerful chap, immaculately dressed, his uniform looked as though it had come out of a band box. He

MIDDLE EAST

never really did a lot of work. I used him to act mainly as an interpreter as I rarely understood what soldiers from Belfast were talking about, but we got on well and he was most respectful to me. But this of course was part of his act.

One Sunday lunchtime he was looking after the shop while I had lunch. I was called to the sick quarters and went in to the duty bunk to find Bill cutting somebody's hair. I said, 'Hey, what's going on?' The sergeant major had suspended him from duty and told the driver to bring me on duty to take over the sick quarters. I was furious and asked him why. He said, 'The sergeant major said I was drunk.' I observed he didn't look drunk and he could hardly cut anyone's hair if he had been, but I had no option but to go into the office and take over and then I phoned the SMO at El Adem to complain about interference by another service. As I was expressing my views to the SMO on the phone, the CSM and his orderly sergeant came in. The SMO told me to stay there and he would sort it out the next day. I turned to the CSM who had listened to this conversation and he said, 'I'd be careful if I was you, sergeant, how you talk about me or question my orders.' I took a deep breath and said: 'Get out of sick quarters. How dare you! This is an RAF camp not the Army.' The look on his face was a picture. You didn't talk to CMSs like that and live. I did that time and to my surprise they turned round and cleared off.

The next morning the SMO went to see the Colonel and then sent for me. He told me that the CSM was charging McCloughlin with being drunk on duty and I was the main witness. I nearly exploded with anger. I was told to shut up, calm down and leave things alone. The charge had to go through and that was that. Bill was now, of course, suspended from duty and after the next morning clinic he came into the office.

'Sorry about that,' he said 'but the CSM came out of the sergeants' mess and he had been drinking also.'

'Prove it!' I demanded. He couldn't and as he was talking he was scratching his leg. I looked down and saw that the skin above his socks was raw and red and asked him what it was.

'Oh, my psoriasis. It's always bad when I'm in trouble and in the desert,' he explained.

I took him into the treatment room and got his clothes off. He was covered with an acute exacerbation of the disease, which was very irritable indeed. I saw the answer to the problem ... The next clinic in Cyprus was the following day and I was able to get him off my pitch on that afternoon's flight from El Adem. I told the army orderly room that he would be going and asked them for his documents; they didn't connect him with the charge the next day, so the case collapsed as there was no accused. We all had a good laugh but the CSM was not amused. McCloughlin returned about four weeks later, after treatment by the dermatologist, a lot better. Nothing more was said about the episode but I did ask Bill if he'd been drunk and he admitted he could hardly hold the scissors when I came into the room. Still, such is life.

About two months later I was called before the SMO. The story had gone as far as Headquarters Middle East Airforce and the AOC was annoyed. I was dressed down for endangering service relationships as was the CSM, but the CSM was a man and he came and found me to apologise. We became the best of friends but I never told him about Bills' high blood alcohol level.

I had now another nursing attendant posted in, which made three staff, so I was able to relax a little, take stock of the situation in which we found ourselves, and make some more necessary improvements. I received a sum of money from the Patients' Comfort Fund, with which I purchased some large lithographs of European scenes, such as gardens and mountains and snowfields, and got the NAAFI odd job man to stick them on huge sheets of ply and put them on the walls of the corridors of sick quarters. This really cheered the place up and I twisted the arm of the MPBW boss and managed to get a new toilet and bath fitted and the bathroom repainted. This took an awful lot of persuasion as fittings like these were like gold dust. I was very proud of my newly decorated bathroom and to start with, wouldn't let anyone clean it apart from myself. The first day I cleaned the toilet, which must have had a flaw in it, I broke the pan with the brush and I looked at the damage in dismay. I had to be very contrite with the boss of MPBW and we had to have a toilet, so it was grudgingly replaced. This was the second toilet I had broken in my service career and in this case it was just due to over-enthusiasm in cleaning. I do like fittings like this to be spotless. If the toilets and fittings are clean in an organisation, then the standard of the rest of the place is usually high, I maintain.

One of my new nursing attendants was a tall gangling lad of about nineteen who was trying to get off with one of the new Salvation Army officers at the Salvation Army Book Shop and to encourage his suit, he decided to do a lay preacher's course run by the Church of Scotland padre. However I never felt very comfortable with this lad, whose name was Livings. He was rather arrogant and wouldn't listen. He didn't impress me but I had no cause to complain about his work as yet.

One day the post arrived at station sick quarters with a large, heavy parcel addressed to him. It was from the British and Foreign Bible Society, obviously books. We had had a few brushes with the Libyan religious authorities and one young man the previous year had been sent home rapidly after preaching in the streets of Tobruk. After all we were in Libya only on tolerance. Libya was a sovereign state with its own rules and this was very provocative ... breaking our terms of reference ... so when I saw the package I could sense trouble.

I sent for him and asked what the contents of the package were but he refused to answer me and when I asked him if they were bibles, he didn't reply. I told him the legal situation, ordered him to open the package and show me but he refused. I had the authority, of course, to arrest him and put in the guard room and prefer charges, but I didn't want to damage his career for a youthful indiscretion.

I told him I was going to see the guard commander and, walking down the road, I fortunately bumped into a senior C of E padre, Wing Commander Patterson and told him of my predicament.

'Well,' he said, 'we can't let him do this. I will come and talk to him.' He asked me if I was sure they were bibles and I said I thought so. So on the way back to the sick quarters, we called in at the unit interpreter, Mr Zenussi, and asked him to come and look at the package on condition that he said no more about it. He agreed and after about 10 minutes the padre who interviewed the lad came out of the office and told him to bring the package with him.

He was then ordered to open it, which he did very reluctantly, and when Mr Zenussi looked at the books, his face went very hard and he snarled,

'Yes, they are Christian holy books and are banned.'

The padre took the book and reminded the lad about his place in the RAF, that he was there to look after airmen's health not the Arab souls, and left with the books. Mr Zenussi was as good as his word and didn't say anything so the affair blew over, but it left me with a surly nursing attendant who was unfortunately the sort of young man who had to have the last word.

One weekend I went on duty to find a large collie dog in the duty room. This was Livings', I was told, and he had the permission of the CO to keep him. I was furious and not at all pleased as he had chucked out the sickquarters cat and put the dog in its place. I spoke to the CO, who confirmed that he could have the dog so long as it wasn't a nuisance. If it was, it would have to go. He had got the dog from a family who were going home and didn't want to put it into quarantine for six months. The next morning there was a terrible row outside the sick-quarters. I ran out of the treatment room to find that the dog had escaped from the duty room and was being attacked by a pack of pi dogs. It then ran into the sick quarters with the pack of dogs chasing behind, scattering the patients. It was the antenatal clinic that morning, with lots of pregnant wives in the building who were petrified but the poor dog was being pulled to pieces by the pi dogs. Eventually we managed to get Livings's dog out of the way, very badly injured with his tail torn off and bleeding from lacerations and what looked like a fractured jaw. The dog was in agony and it was impossible to do anything about it so after consultation with the CO, he said, 'Well, you had better put him down.' Livings was not very pleased when he arrived the next day but the young man had caused a lot of disruption in my sick quarters and I wanted no more of it. I interviewed him the next day and got a promise of good behaviour out of him or next time he would be for the high jump.

I had another nursing attendant, a youngster called Swain, who was quite the opposite sort of personality. He was quiet and respectful and gave the impression of being a bit dim. However, his hobby was martial arts and he held a black belt in judo. He worked well in sick quarters and the patients seemed to like him but he had trouble off duty – the lad had to sleep in a billet with the army personnel.

There had been a change of regiment and we now had a couple of companies from one of the County Regiments, the Sherwood Foresters. Most of their men were hard men and rather arrogant and the adjutant, with whom I had fallen out on a matter of protocol, was like this too. He was the grandson of the colonel of the regiment and he hoped eventually to fill this prestigious post. He said to me one day, 'You don't like the Army, do you sergeant?' I replied that the Army was fine; it was the people in it who were the trouble. He had no sense of humour.

However, Swain was getting a lot of stick from a couple of these squaddies, who were calling him a fairy and so on. This term was very common even in the RAF; they all thought we were a bit soft or queer in the medical branch until of course they were ill, and Swain had taken quite a lot of abuse. One night about midnight I was called to the guardroom to see three casualties. Two army men, one with a bruised arm and one with bruises on his face and chest. I checked them out and gave them first aid. They were okay. They had been involved in a fight, I was told, and they were in the cells pending a charge of unruly behaviour. The other lad in the other cell turned out to be Swain. He was fine but had bruised knuckles.

'What happened?' I asked. He told me that these two had

started on him with taunts and were interfering with his locker. He warned them and eventually told them he was a judo black belt and that made them even more taunting and abrasive. Unfortunately for them, Swain lost his temper, picked them both up and chucked them at the wall.

'Good for you,' I smiled, 'That will teach them! Still, you will be charged, you know.' He was fined, his sentence ameliorated because of continual provocation, and the two soldiers were fined and their privileges stopped for two weeks. After that, Swain was left alone. At least Swain didn't get a dog!

The next brush with the animal kingdom came with Major Crane, the Salvation Army officer of the book shop, with whom I had also crossed swords about something in the past. She phoned me up and asked me to look at a dog which had been injured. It was rather like Livings's collie and quite an old dog and again, unfortunately, had got out of the compound and had been very badly savaged by the pi dogs. Could I help? I examined the poor beast and he was indeed very badly injured, his lower jaw torn away and bleeding profusely.

'Sorry,' I said, 'I can't repair that without an anaesthetic and we have no equipment for veterinary work. There is one thing I can do and that is put her down.'

Very reluctantly she agreed to let me do this so I mixed up my drugs and, after I had injected the poor old thing, she was dead within 15 seconds. I offered to take her away but she wanted to bury the dog in the compound. So I stood up and packed my syringe and bits and pieces away and said,

'Okay, that will be £1.50 please, Mrs Crane.'

She looked at me outraged.

'What?' she said 'You charge?'

'Come on. A labourer is worthy of his hire.' I quoted.

She went to the till, crashed it open, dug out £1.50 and thrust it into my hands. I took the money and put it straight away into a self-denial box on the counter. She looked at the box and then looked at me.

'What did you do that for?' she asked.

'Major Crane, you asked me to do something that you couldn't do yourself. I asked to be paid and you objected but I stuck to my guns and made you pay. The money then became mine and now you're questioning what I do with my own money. I find that offensive!' After that she calmed down and we became the best of friends. She was quite a character, that lady, but under her somewhat chilling exterior she had a heart of gold.

I had more adventures with animals, mainly due to accidents. One day a pi dog got into the school grounds and the Arab caretaker injured it badly. I was called to this poor animal, which was roaming around the school playground snarling and attacking anybody who approached it. The police managed to catch it and in the end brought it to me, but we couldn't get near it. We tied it up with a rope in the courtyard at the back of sick quarters and it was roaming around on about 10 feet of rope – any approach to it resulted in a violent attack on the person. Obviously we had to sedate it somehow in order to dispose of it. It would have been cruel to let it go back into town, knowing the way the Arab children would have treated it. As it was bleeding badly, I sent my corporal to the NAAFI to buy some dog food and when after an hour or so it would be hungry, we planned to give it the food with about ten sleeping tablets in it. This we did but it made not the slightest bit of difference to the animal, so I waited again for an hour and doubled the dose. After a couple of hours or so it was calming down and we discussed what to do.

It was still not fully unconscious and any approach, however quiet, made the dog stand up groggily, growl and show his very nasty fangs. We decided to recruit another couple of airmen to give us a hand. I got a counterpane from the cupboard. I planned we would each take a corner and very slowly walk towards the dog and, when the counterpane was right over it, we would lower it down on the dog. Standing on each corner, we could then walk towards the dog, secure it and then I could inject through the counterpane. So we started, got the counterpane over the dog, let it down and then I said,

'Okay now, chaps, start walking towards the dog.' Now at

that very moment the dog woke up. 'Come on, chaps.' I said. 'Chaps!'

I looked round. They had all gone, leaving me with the ferocious animal charging around mixed up with the counterpane. I retreated hurriedly to think up Plan B. However after another half hour the poor thing started to succumb to the sleeping pills and eventually became unconscious, whereupon I was able to inject it and put it out of its misery.

Another problem was cats. They were very difficult to deal with and they knew you had an evil intent towards them. I insisted that any cat brought to me to be put down was in a box or some other strong container, so that we had some control over it. One afternoon one of the civilian school teachers phoned me to say his cat had become diabetic and had become quite ill. Would I kindly put it out of its misery? He was a nice man and very upset about this so I agreed and asked him to bring it along. He arrived with the cat in his arms and I could hear the row it was making from inside the sick quarters. When I went to the door and opened it, Mr W. was having quite a job keeping hold of the animal.

'He wouldn't go inside a box,' he explained.

The cat seemed to know what was happening so I got my corporal to get hold of the animal and we took it into the treatment room where I had my material ready. The easiest way to do it was to drop the cat into a large cardboard box which contained a sizeable cotton wool swab soaked in chloroform. When the cat had been dropped into the box and the box sealed with sticking plaster, I put some nitrous oxide gas inside, displacing the oxygen rapidly, and the animal normally went to sleep and was despatched remarkably quickly and perfectly safely. This time I had everything ready. I told the corporal to hold it over the box and to drop it in when I said so. As he did so the animal turned over in the air, opened his jaws as wide as I have ever seen a cat do since and clamped them on my left thigh, pumping away with his rear legs onto my right thigh. There was blood everywhere. I was shouting and trying to get the animal off.

MIDDLE EAST

The corporal stood there white-faced and didn't know what to do when suddenly the cat leapt off me, flew across the room, crashing straight through the window and it was gone. After I had patched myself up with a bit of help, the phone rang. Mr West said that the cat had come home. I asked him if he still wanted me to put it down and he said he did, so I asked him please to bring the cat in a box this time. He arrived some half an hour later with the cat in a Lloyd Loom dirty linen basket. That was better so this time we put the box with the cat in it into the big cardboard box with a whole bottle of chloroform, sealed it up, squirted in the gas and left it alone. Resisting the temptation to see what had happened, I left it for half an hour and then opened the box. Oh dear, the basket was not a wicker one, it was made of plastic and it had melted completely in the chloroform. And there, cocooned in a molten mass of plastic, was the dead cat.

Another commitment I had was to turn out for accidents and incidents at sea. The Marine Craft Section had a large 64-foot pinnace with large Rolls Royce Sea Griffon engines and an inflatable boat with a powerful outboard engine. Every now and again exercises were held, usually a simulated rescue or some other event, but one day a call was received from the marine craft section to say that a Royal Navy supply ship was in the harbour which had a severe casualty on board following a major storm at sea. It had limped into port early one morning listing badly. The captain had fallen against a stanchion and apparently had injured his chest and was in great pain.

I was taken out to the ship, which had a rope ladder down the side, and I climbed up some 20–30 feet to the deck above. The boat was listing at some 15 degrees and it was very difficult to keep one's feet but I found the captain on his back in his cabin in his bunk. He had fractured about six ribs on his right side and though fortunately these had not punctured his lung, he was nevertheless in great pain and was unable to help himself. He was an older grey-haired man and was very, very cross with himself and indeed with everybody else. I had to calm him down and it was obvious I would be unable to take him off the ship without the use of a proper stretcher, which could cope with someone who had a fracture. I gave him a sedative and went back to the sick quarters to get the stretcher but, thinking about the problem, I chickened out and went into the office to ask Taff, my corporal, if he would like a trip out (as he didn't get many) to collect the chap and take him to hospital at El Adem. He jumped at the chance and ran off happily, collected the stretcher and went down to the Marine Craft Section in the ambulance to do the job.

I thought that would be the last I would see of him for a few hours and settled down in the office to do a bit of paper work. To my great surprise, Taff was back in about an hour.

'Where's the patient?' I asked.

'In hospital, of course!' he said.

'So how did you get him over the side into the boat?'

'No trouble,' he replied.

'Well how did you get him down the rope ladder?' I asked out of curiosity.

'I didn't', he said nonchalantly, 'I took the boat round the other side of the ship where it was level with the water, and we just stepped over the side into the inflatable.'

Oh dear, I still cringe when thinking about it after all these years. The Marine Craft Section was busy all that summer and needed the services of the Medical Branch often.

On the day before my main summer leave in Malta, I went up early in the morning to collect my leave money from the accounts section at El Adem. We were never paid the full amount each week, so I had put some pay by for such things as emergencies and annual leave. I had collected some 500 Libyan pounds, about £650 sterling. I arrived home to my flat at about 1200 hours and as I was about to go into my bedroom to change, the warning sirens sounded from the Marine Craft Section. I dashed out of the flat, jumped into my car and headed down to the docks. By the time I had got there, having been caught up in the usual Arab traffic, I saw the pinnace leaving the harbour mouth. The inflatable was waiting for me and I jumped into it with all my kit and off we went at a rate of knots. It was very

MIDDLE EAST

rough, with quite a wind blowing and it was not until we were about four miles out in the open sea that we caught up with the pinnace. We came alongside and I boarded the pinnace and was told that a Greek T33 trainer had ditched and a box search was taking place to locate the two missing airmen. After about half an hour we found these two bedraggled specimens, pulled them aboard and took them down to the small sick bay under the wheelhouse, where I checked them out, covered them and warmed them up. They had no injuries but were very frightened and very cold. Even in warm weather in the Mediterranean, sea immersion is very cooling. We turned back to the harbour and an hour later we arrived, offloaded the airmen into an ambulance, and sent them to hospital at El Adem with one of my nursing attendants in charge.

I cleared up the mess in the sick quarters and went up to the Captain to report off. As I stood chatting with him, I put my hands into my pockets and found that my wallet with the £500 Libyan was missing! I must have gone white because he said,

'Whatever is the matter?'

I told him I had lost my wallet. It must have fallen out of my pocket as I climbed up into the pinnace from the inflatable. Straightaway he put a guard on the gangplank, stopping anybody going ashore and called the RAF police to check the boat. Nothing was found but the crew were all questioned and I was the most unpopular chap. After about half an hour it was obvious that I had lost my wallet. It was not on the pinnace, therefore it was probably at the bottom of the Mediterranean. It was now late and impossible to get up to pay accounts and get a loan, even if that had been possible that day.

We were booked on an early morning flight from El Adem to Malta and were meeting my in-laws for a three-week holiday on that island the next morning. I was in despair. Totally wet from the incident, I drove home, parked the car despondently and rang the bell. My wife answered the door.

'You're wet!' she said as if I didn't know it. 'Why did you go out without your wallet and ID card?'

'Oh dear, another clanger,' I thought. 'Whenever I have anything to do with Marine Craft Section, I do something like this.'

There was obviously a great need to re-establish myself quickly in the eyes of the Marine Craft people so I went straight up to the mess and found Paddy the mess steward. We were rationed in those days to 2 cans of lager a day but I asked him for two crates of 24 each and he refused point blank. I twisted his arm and suggested that after the number of times I had bent the rules for him he had no option but to relent and let me have them.

Back to the Marine Craft Section I went, with the booze, through the gate guard and knocked on the door of the crew room, which was opened by one of the chaps.

'Oh, it's you!' he said sullenly.

I was obviously very unpopular. I pushed the two crates of booze through the door and shouted,

'I found it!' and ran off before anything else happened to me.

There was a great cheer from inside so all was well that ended well and the next day we went off and had three fabulous weeks in Malta, which island Mark Twain, the American comedian, called the biggest heap of stones in the Mediterranean! This was my first visit to the island and how we did enjoy it!

On my return, I found that the work had piled up and as usual it took about two weeks to clear the backlog of bits and pieces that accrue in running a Section in the Air Force and it was now also drawing towards the cooler months.

I had been back from holiday for about a week when one Sunday afternoon the ambulance driver arrived at the flat to say that a child had fallen down a ventilation shaft and appeared to be very badly injured. I got to the scene in about five minutes, to find a crowd of locals and RAF families gathered round one of the ventilation shafts. These went right into the ground to some old submarine workshops built into the cliff top by the harbour. The shafts had been wired off but one of our children, a ten year old, the son of a sergeant fitter on the patch, had been exploring, had slipped down the shaft and had missed his footing. They could

MIDDLE EAST

hear him now, calling and crying a long way below but you couldn't see anything.

I do hate holes in the ground. I could never be a potholer and for me this really was a nightmare scenario but down I had to go. I sent the ambulance back to the fire section for ropes and lights and armed with my torch, started the descent. There was a platform about 20 feet down reached by rungs in a vertical shaft and another shaft led down from this for another 30 feet or so. The rungs were all old and loose and rusty but I gritted my teeth and continued down in pitch darkness into a large ruined workshop below. At the foot of the shaft the child was lying, very frightened and tearful with an obvious fractured right femur and cuts to his arm and head; he was pretty shocked and cold by this time. Fortunately the fire section arrived quickly.

I called for a couple of chaps to come down with some blankets and ropes and lights and bring my major incident kit, which was kept in the ambulance. The boy was in a lot of pain and the first task was to put up a drip and get him sedated before we could splint his leg and move him. One of the firemen I used as a runner to go up and phone the MO and get permission to use a small dose of morphine to settle him down. By now the SMO had arrived from the nearby beach and he stayed at the top and gave me permission, via the fireman, to use any necessary drugs. And so the sergeant and myself started work on him.

When the child was stable and we'd got him splinted and on a stretcher, we had to think of how to get him out. It would have been impossible to go up the shaft; it was too narrow, so the runner and another chap were told to look for another way out. Finally they returned and said that they had found another passageway through which we could probably get to the harbour. We made our way out eventually to the cliff face, which was about 15 feet above the water. By this time the boy was asleep but we managed to get out onto the cliff face. This was vertical but we gradually eased him up to the waiting ambulance, which then transported him to the local hospital at El Adem. We had collected his parents by this time and I reassured them. Within the hour he was 'casevaced' to Cyprus with his mother in attendance.

It was a wonder to me that I had done it. I hate holes in the ground and the next day I went back to have a look at the scene as a matter of curiosity. I could recognise nothing; my mind had gone onto auto pilot and we had just got on with it. It was wonderful that everything went so well and great credit was due to the fire section that the rescue had been so smooth. Their efforts were rewarded with a 'well-done' certificate from the Air Officer Commanding.

There was another difficult episode a little while later when I was called out one wet Wednesday afternoon. We had had some unseasonal rain and drizzle for a couple of days. I arrived at an address on the far side of town after having been called by a lady who was concerned by the behaviour of her neighbour. She told me that the lady next door was behaving strangely and wouldn't answer her door, but if I came into her patio, I could climb a ladder and look over into the woman's patio and probably get down and sort the problem out. The woman's husband was on duty in El Adem and she had been alone for some 24 hours.

I climbed up the ladder and there down below me the woman was standing naked in the rain holding a large cook's knife in her hands and scratching the word 'hate' on the wall of the patio. I looked down and told the ambulance driver to go back to station sick quarters, phone the SMO for advice and bring a couple of policemen to help. They arrived within five minutes with a note from the SMO, which said I should give her 5ccs of paraldehyde, a potent sedative.

'Thank you very much!' I said. 'That's all I need! How do I do that?'

The policemen then suggested that they break in and then wrap blankets around their arms and hold her down so that I could inject her. I went up to the ladder first of all and tried to talk to her but she didn't listen and either couldn't or wouldn't hear. Eventually we had to break into the house. She was fighting mad when she saw the policemen. I opened the ampoule and

MIDDLE EAST

drew the drug up into the syringe. The policemen restrained her so that I could inject her and I went to pick up the syringe but unfortunately the syringe was plastic and had melted with the paraldehyde.

There were panic stations, she was going berserk and she had already escaped from the policemen once. They captured her again and so I had to draw up very quickly another dose of the drug and rapidly inject before this one melted. This I did but it was a very close run thing (the syringe collapsed but I got most of it in) and within ten minutes she was calming down and we managed to get her on to a stretcher, into the ambulance, and then on our way to El Adem. It was quite a journey and she tried to climb out of the window even though she was sedated. I had to put straps round her but she was very confused and, with the drug, if she had got free she would have been very dangerous. I was very glad indeed when we arrived at the hospital in El Adem. Unfortunately she reacted very badly to the plastic of the syringe and she ended up with a massive urticarial rash all over her which lasted for 24 hours.

I had to go back to Tobruk that evening and went into the guardroom to thank the policemen for their help. They showed me a book she had been reading; it had a lurid cover with a big cook's knife depicted on it and was entitled *Death in the Rain*. It must have triggered her attack. Subsequently, however, I learnt that she had had psychiatric problems in the past, so she had to be repatriated to the UK as soon as possible.

Some time later we went on holiday to Cyrene in the Jebel Akbar, which means the Green Mountains. This was a small mountain range about 60 miles long, 2 miles from the coast and 150 miles from Tobruk. The army at Benghazi had a couple of caravans which they hired out to the families and we spent a very happy time exploring the ruins of the great Roman city of Cyrene and the necropolis. The only fly in the ointment was that our daughter, then aged 5 years old, would not use the Elsan and spent the whole week with tummy ache. It was quite a fantastic week, however. We had the whole city to ourselves. No tourists

The children leaning on my very cheap Ford Cortina.

visited the area in those days and we were able to walk around and poke about in all the corners of ancient rooms, buildings and houses and see all the sights. Arab children sometimes followed us from the local village and tried to sell ancient coins that they had dug up for a few piastres, but apart from that it was deserted and was a photographic delight.

I was now getting used to photography. I had a small Kodak Coloursnap camera which did quite a good job; the light, of course, was so good in the desert that it was difficult to take bad photographs. A number of my slides were commented on by various people when I showed them, and I was encouraged to enter a photographic competition in which I won second prize and was highly commended for some of my shots.

One day the CO phoned me to come down to his office. He had had a letter from a man in Solihull who had been in Tobruk during the siege in 1942 and had heard a talk on the radio about Tobruk garrison. He had not realised that we still had a garrison in place and he asked the CO if he would send him a picture of the

Tobruk garrison as it was today. The CO asked me if I would take care of it as he knew I was interested in photography, and send him a few pictures. He seemed to be a nice chap by the way he wrote and I went out and shot off a couple of films, 36 exposures of Tobruk and area, and sent them to him. Two weeks later he wrote back absolutely delighted and asking whether I could get him some shots of various other locations which he detailed. I sent about four of these films and each time followed a most grateful letter of thanks. One day came the sixty-four thousand dollar question: would I send him a photograph of his friend's grave in the war cemetery? He gave me his friend's number, rank and name and told me they had been strafed by a Junkers 88. His comrade, a flight sergeant, had been killed outright. He had buried him at the side of the El Adem road, as he thought it was.

I went to Tobruk and to the Knightsbridge cemeteries but there was no sign of his name in the book so I contacted the War Graves people at Benghazi. They searched all the records but he was not there and they advised me to write back to the chap and get the true location and they would try and find his body and bring him there for a proper burial. This was of course 1967 and they were still coming across dead soldiers who had been buried in shallow graves during hostilities. The sand had blown off the graves over the years and the desiccated bodies were given a proper burial with full military honours. So I wrote to him requesting details but heard no more and forgot about him.

When two months later a letter did arrive, it was from his widow. He had died of a heart attack and she wrote to tell me that since the War he had been a semi-permanent invalid and for the last few weeks he had been utterly happy poring over my photographs; it had given him such a lot of pleasure. She said she was deeply grateful for what I had done for him but as for my question about his friend, she had no knowledge. She said that part of her husband's life was private and he never spoke about it at all, so she couldn't help. It's amazing what does go on behind people's closed doors and how often and unwittingly one can influence a life for better or for worse by one's actions. At least I had made his last few weeks a bit more tolerable and for that I was very grateful.

It was now the winter of 1967 and just before Christmas the weather had broken. One evening a flight of Hunter jets was exercising high above Tobruk when two collided in thick cloud. One badly damaged aircraft managed to limp back to El Adem and land safely but the other pilot had to eject and parachuted into the sea some five miles off the coast. The pinnace left about 7.00 with one of our medical officers on board to recover the pilot. I was busy at the time with a casualty in the sick quarters. When they returned at midnight, having found nobody, the search and rescue beacon on the pilot's lifejacket was still signalling somewhere out in the darkness. I arrived at the Marine Craft Section at around midnight, really as a matter of curiosity and to see what was going on, just as the pinnace returned for refuelling.

The MO had gone home to tell his wife he would be out all night when suddenly there was a hole in the weather. Up till then it had been raining heavily and a six to seven gale-force wind had been blowing from the west. Then the wind suddenly changed and, as the MO hadn't yet returned, the CO ordered me aboard instead and off we went. It was very rough and when it stopped raining, a sandstorm started blowing from the south making visibility poor, so it was pretty uncomfortable. The beacon was still transmitting but the signal was weaker. The CO then realised that as the signal was weakening, we were going 180 degrees in the wrong direction and we turned about and headed east in the direction of the Egyptian waters. This was not a happy situation as Colonel Nasser in those days didn't like us very much and it would have been difficult to arrange a rescue in his waters.

We ploughed on until first light with the signal growing louder and as the sun came up we saw, about two miles ahead, a bright orange inflatable life raft but as we came closer to it, we could see that it was empty. This was a grave disappointment. We felt sick at heart but we picked up the dinghy. Suddenly, on the horizon, we could see a large tug, the sort that was used to tow the tankers into the oil terminal, signalling that she had the pilot on board. The CO closed on the tug, which looked like a block of flats towering above us in this heaving sea. One minute we were looking down at the deck the next minute looking up at it.

'There you are!' he said to me 'You will have to go over. Put on your life jacket.'

I had never been so scared in my life. I could see myself being crushed between the two boats.

'Stand on the side of the pinnace,' he said 'And don't let go until I tell you. When I say go, walk onto the tug!'

He manoeuvred the pinnace into position and as we went into a great trough of the sea, he told me to get ready. When we came up, he said, 'Go when I tap your shoulder,' and I just stepped across onto the tug, which hurtled me up in the air with the pinnace now far below me. It was easy! I picked myself up, grabbed my medical kit and staggered up towards the bridge. The first officer opened the door. I stepped into another world, quiet and orderly, with half a dozen officers in beautiful smart doe skin uniforms, completely civilised. It was a German tug; of course it had to be. And me in my wet soggy RAF khaki drill uniform looking like a tramp! I saluted the Captain.

'Good morning,' he said, 'I have your pilot in a bunk down below. Would you like to go with the first officer to see him?'

Well, the pilot was okay – just shaken up and rather bruised and tired – I gave him a sedative after I had examined him and settled him down. When he was asleep, I went back to the bridge.

'Could I use your radio?' I asked the Captain. I could get no reply from the pinnace; the radio on it had gone u/s. of course.

'Can I have a loud hailer?' I asked.

I went out onto the wing of the bridge and reported through the loud hailer. The skipper on the pinnace requested that I brought the injured pilot over.

'Not a good idea,' said I. 'I have sedated him.'

I didn't fancy taking the poor chap over by a line in that sea and then dropping him again into the water, so the skipper said he would follow us back to the harbour. Just then one of the engines of the pinnace went u/s. I was really beginning to feel a little bit ashamed of our own efforts. However, the steward came up to the bridge on the captain's request and invited me to breakfast. So I sat in their wardroom, eating bacon and eggs and looking out on our poor boat labouring in heavy seas beside us. It was worth the harrowing journey from the pinnace to the tug just for the bacon and egg. We offloaded the pilot some three hours later. He was none the worse for his adventures but no doubt had a few questions to answer to a board of enquiry some days later concerning the loss of his aircraft.

One of my weekly chores was to go to El Adem in the ambulance for stores. We couldn't keep a vast amount of medicines at Tobruk as we had only a small refrigerated store and, in the heat, drugs soon lost their potency. One week, however, my eldest boy had developed a very bad earache for which there was no apparent reason so I took both my sons with me for a ride. The ENT surgeon was over from Cyprus for a week looking at patients. My son was seen by the surgeon and I had collected my drugs and medicines and was ready to go when the air field alarm sounded. The warrant officer in charge of the station Sick Headquarters phoned the tower and asked what the problem was and they requested help.

The barrier at the end of the runway worked like a railway crossing with two arms one either side of the runway, which lifted up a large nylon net between them. It was used to prevent an aircraft, if it lost its brakes or its reverse thrust didn't work, from overshooting the runway and hurtling off into the desert. This had failed; one of the arms wouldn't rise because a large snake had crawled into the mechanism and was fouling the works. Could we help? The junior medical officer went and got some permanganate of potash and sulphuric acid from the stores and we all went out in the ambulance, my two boys as well, to try and smoke the creature out.

Two hunter aircraft were in the circuit and couldn't land until the net was down and they only had sixteen minutes of fuel left. The barrier mechanism was in a stand about four feet high with

MIDDLE EAST

the arm attached to it at the top coming out of a metal bell housing which covered the works like a tin hat. The snake had crawled into this housing and any amount of prodding by the ground crew just annoyed it and drew forth the most violent hissing and bumping. The MO got out his chemicals, mixed the two together in a glass dish and pushed the dish onto the ground under the bell housing. A great cloud of smoke was emitted from this hell brew but unfortunately the wind was too strong and blew most of it away. Now back to square one, so I thought I should add my pennyworth. I took the shovel from the side of the ambulance and very courageously or stupidly, crept up to the bell and gave it an enormous bang with the shovel. The snake, being quite sensitive to sound, was stunned. It dropped out onto the ground, rested for a second then turned round and went off into the desert at a rate of knots. I had no idea that snakes could move so fast. It seemed to be about five feet long and quite thick. It went for about 50 yards, stopped, turned round and came back at me like an express train. I ran and jumped into the ambulance as it shot round the vehicle with everyone running out of its way and went straight back into the bell housing, obviously time for plan B.

We now knew how to dislodge it so this time I asked the MO to get the pyrene fire extinguisher from the side of the ambulance. I would bang on the bell housing again and if the snake then fell out he was to squirt the noxious substance at it to confuse it and I would clobber it with the shovel. Amazingly enough this worked. It was pretty scary but everything else had failed and we couldn't think of anything else to do. Both my boys were watching this wide-eyed from the ambulance. My youngest son lived on the story for weeks afterwards and each time he told it – my dad killed a snake – the snake got bigger. So life was full of surprises.

I was enjoying life but sometimes we had scares which reminded us how serious life really was. One of our families had a delightful little girl about four years old. She was pretty and petite, both parents were attractive people, both civilian teachers at the school, the child was a sheer delight and they rarely had to visit Station Sick Quarters. Furthermore, the mother was a trained nurse and didn't really trust the medical profession, preferring to treat her family with her own remedies. One evening I was called to go down to their house; the child was not well. In fact when I got there I couldn't really say what was wrong. But she was fretful and I thought she could have had a urinary tract infection. This could be most unpleasant in the heat; even in winter the temperature sometimes went up to 80 degrees F and urinary tract infections were common in children if they wouldn't drink a lot – but this somehow seemed different.

She was too listless and toxic and I was worried. I wanted to take her straight away to El Adem to see the Senior Medical Officer, who was good with children. Her mother said she would rather I didn't – would I give them some Calpol for the child? I preferred to talk to the SMO first so after I had examined the child, I went up to Station Sick Quarters to telephone and on the way called in at the mess for my mail. In the post was a letter from my mother-in-law to say that my niece, aged two years old, had just died from meningitis, having been unwell for only two hours. This frightened me. I turned straight round without bothering to phone the SMO and went back to the house and demanded that the child came to the hospital without fail or I would have to inform the civilian liaison commanding officer. It was quite a nasty situation but in the end, after a bit of bullying, she complied and I got the child to hospital. On the way the child had a fit and I was relieved when we arrived and she was admitted.

She was discharged some three days later. No-one knew what was wrong with her, it must have been a viral infection but I went to see the mother and father and apologised for my behaviour. When I explained to them what had happened, they saw it differently and apologised to me and we became the best of friends thereafter.

So life continued – incident after incident, never a dull minute – until one day the Six-Day War started between the Israelis and the Arabs and life took a step backwards. We were all placed under

My friend Sgt. Major Ali, Chief of the traffic police in Tobruk.

curfew and the town became deserted apart from mobs of local youths gathering and shouting slogans and marching. It was a very difficult time because I still had to work, but the CO of the local traffic police was very helpful. I had done a number of jobs, as I have mentioned before, for him and his family and he really appreciated it. I asked for his help this time. My car outside and the ambulance driving around town were vulnerable, but I still had to visit patients. He promised me that we would be safe and he was as good as his word. When an Arab youth threw a stone at my ambulance, the youth was arrested and put inside for a week.

Slowly the mood of the locals changed over the six days from absolute despair as the Israelis triumphed and the Egyptians quickly sued for peace. The Libyan army, of course, had been mobilised; a number of divisions moved up to the Egyptian border, coming through Tobruk, to help the Egyptians, but their help was refused while the King still had British forces on his soil. The poor Libyans, not understanding military adventures, ran out of water and supplies even before they got to the border and were stranded.

By the end of that week the writing was on the wall for the King and we were told to pack our belongings into crates and be ready for immediate evacuation by air or sea. We sat indoors when we were off duty; there was a very quiet and sullen atmosphere in the town. It all fizzled out however, as the history books tell, but life was never the same again and I was getting near my repatriation day in July. We began to think about home and finding accommodation there.

Some six weeks before I was due home, I thought about my car. I could have taken it home but I had done 18,000 really hard miles in it and I didn't think it would be a good idea. The NAAFI manager asked me one day if he could buy it and told me to name a price. I asked him to make me an offer and he offered me 400 pounds.

'Sterling or Libyan?' I asked.

He said Libyan so, for the first time in my life, I had made a profit in selling a car. I had had it for two years and bought it for 400 sterling and sold it for 500 sterling. We had to walk for the last month, much to my wife's annoyance, but with an offer like that I couldn't refuse. So when July came, we packed up and, after the usual hassle on the journey home, we arrived at Lyneham about 24 months after I had left. I was tired; I hadn't realised how tired we all were, but as a posting it had been the best in my service career.

CHAPTER EIGHT

Ely Hospital

I was now due for some four weeks' leave and some two weeks' accumulated annual leave and we spent it at my in-laws at Henlow again. I had sent my brother's brother-in-law a cheque for £400 from Tobruk and asked him to get me a car. He had a garage in the West of England and he had a car waiting for me at Lyneham, so we had transport straight away. Unfortunately my new unit was RAF Hospital, Ely and it had very few married quarters. After the stress and very hard work of living in such a dusty old place, my wife was most unhappy about having nowhere decent to go to. She told the Families Office what she thought about it but this didn't help, of course. All they did was offer me the local paper so I could look for some rented accommodation – this was a good start.

The two boys had won scholarships to the local grammar school five miles from Ely. The time was passing and we needed to be settled by September so that they could start. One of the administration clerks in the hospital gave me the address of a company in Soham, whose owner, a managing director, had spent some time as a patient in the RAF Hospital Ely and felt he owed the hospital a debt of gratitude, which he paid by helping the staff. Apparently a life-saving operation had returned him to good health and he continued to work. His daughter, Mrs Day, acted as the company secretary and turned out to be a most agreeable lady. They helped us enthusiastically and tried to find us some accommodation.

This did prove very difficult at the time, for it was 1968. There was little new housing on the market and thus a great shortage of rentable properties. She did, however, take us to see a cottage five miles out in the country and a mobile home which had no services. She was apologetic about all of this but quite frankly neither would have been any good because both were unfurnished and we only had the minimum of goods to put in them: articles such as the television, radio, washing machine, things which had been in store while we had been away.

The hospital was worse than useless in helping us and it was within a week of my returning to work that I went down to see Mrs Day again in desperation and she thought a tenant on her own caravan site would be leaving the next week. Would we like to move into a fitted mobile home? This we had to accept but by Friday before the Monday's deadline the tenant had decided to stay. Mrs Day then bought for us an ex-holiday caravan from the coast and said it would be available for us on the Sunday – it would be put on the site. This was agreed and, as it was something definite, on the Sunday afternoon we arrived at Soham to take over this caravan, which had not yet arrived. There we were on the pavement with our suitcases and in despair. Mrs Day said, 'Well, it's coming sometime.'

Within the hour a low-loader appeared with a large mobile home on board and it was sited and we moved in. We had to borrow blankets and pillows from Mrs Day but she helped us with everything she could and we settled down to make the best of a bad job.

To say the least, it was extremely unsatisfactory, but we got the boys to their new school on time the next day and I started out at the hospital on a new experience. I was put on an orthopaedic ward. I knew little about orthopaedics and again a lot of learning was needed but I was glad to be back in a hospital environment again. The caravan, though, was proving to be a difficult place to live in, with no running water and a toilet over the yard. Within two weeks the previous caravan that Mrs Day had promised us became vacant and we moved into this on the site proper, with all the mod. cons. It was a lot more comfortable. The following Sunday I took the boys to Evensong at St. Andrews, the local parish church, and was welcomed warmly. The next day the Vicar's wife came to see my wife at the caravan and within a few days we were integrated into the community.

After about six to eight weeks, a rather ramshackle furnished flat became available in the old vicarage next to the church and we changed our venue again, after which life became much better. It wasn't up to much but the owner, a local church warden, was again most helpful so we settled down for another two years and made the best of it, turning it into a home.

The church became the focal point of our lives. The choir was missing a tenor and two sopranos, so I and my two boys fitted in and became part of the life of the church. I was invited to become a server of the communion service and after confirmation of my wife and myself by the Bishop of Huntingdon, I took the post and found as much interest in the spiritual side of people's lives as I had had in the past in their physical and mental problems.

We had now been at Soham for some four months and the boys were settling well at school. The grammar school was rather an old institution but got good results and had high levels of entries into the universities and the professions, and I hoped this would help my two lads. However it was rather parochial, being in the depth of the Fens, and had reasonably large class sizes. Unfortunately, both my lads, having been to an RAF school, had been used to no more than 15 to a class and in my eldest son's second year only twelve had been in his class. Therefore, although he was very bright, he found himself in competition with a number of children of his own age from a somewhat broader social background. He was, however, quite used to expressing himself and could do so remarkably well, being an articulate youngster. He then fell foul of the deputy headmaster, who was an ex-RAF Wing Commander educator during the war.

At the first Parents Teacher Association we attended I had just come off duty and was still in uniform when this rather superior figure, who was also Graham's form tutor, told me that Graham talked too much. I asked him if what he said was of any value or was nonsense. A lot of it was irrelevant, he said, and usually about his adventures abroad; civilian children in that part of the world in the Fens in those years rarely went as far as Yarmouth. So they didn't really understand him but the teacher should have done so. I pointed out that he had been warned by myself and his mother that he would now be a small fish in a big pond and could not become top every time. I'm not sure whether this man heard what I had said but he replied very nastily: 'Oh you are the sort of parent that wants your children to be better than the others, are you?'

I looked him straight in the face and said,

'He has learnt a lot since he has been at this grammar school and he has learnt well.'

'And what's that?' asked the teacher.

'He doesn't like you!' I replied. The poor man didn't know what to say and went to talk to somebody else. People just didn't talk to him like that. Apart from this, the boys did well and were happy and we were reasonably content in Soham and now settled.

At this stage I was thinking of applying for a tutor's course at last. I knew that if I did, we would be settled for quite a long while. And so we started more enquiries about house purchase to consolidate our position. My bank manager, however, was not enthusiastic and so, unfortunately, we shelved this and later regretted it.

I was on night duty over Christmas until after the New Year. The in-laws had stayed with us over the holiday and went back just before January. As I drove home, on the radio that morning came the New Years Honours List. I thought, 'Well, what have they done? They didn't work as hard as I did in Tobruk for a couple of years and most of them either played football or pranced around on the stage – this was hardly a recommendation for honours. However, I forgot about it and went to bed. When I went on duty that evening, to my surprise I was handed a signal from Headquarters Support Command. It was a telegram from the Air Officer in Chief congratulating me on my award.

'What award?' I asked.

Nobody seemed to know. So the next morning before I went home I looked at the *Daily Telegraph* and there was my name in

Author getting the B.E.M. from the A.O.C. in C at Bentley Priory H.Q., 11 Group, March 1959.

the military honours. I had been awarded a British Empire Medal for my services in the medical branch in Tobruk. I had already had an Air Officer Commanding Commendation in Tobruk and an Air Officer Commanding-in-Chief Commendation before I came home, so the words of the med. sec. officer who had said to me two years previously, 'Stay there and you will be all right' had been true. I was immensely pleased with this and was able to sew a pink and white medal ribbon on my uniform, which looked very nice. I was very proud of it. A few weeks later I was invested with the medal at Headquarters 11 Group at Bentley Priory. My wife and eldest son came with me and we were treated royally for the day.

Work on the orthopaedic division was really very hard but most satisfying. We dealt with a lot of civilian patients as well as our own, and did a lot of reconstructive surgery. The ward sister in the department, Sheila Firth, was a highly qualified orthopaedic nurse and what she didn't know about orthopaedics wasn't worth knowing. She was a very straight and honest lady; she had a sense of humour even if she didn't always show it. However we got on thoroughly well. Some of our cases were very complicated and victims of road and air accidents needed a lot of support. She was never sentimental about it. These patients needed help, not our sympathy, she said. I knew just what she meant. It was easy to get bogged down emotionally, as I had found when dealing with bad burn patients in Halton in 1964.

One particularly sad case was admitted one night soon after my arrival, a 34 year-old family man who had lost his wife, brother-in-law and two of his three children in a massive road traffic accident just outside Cambridge on the Ely road. He had numerous minor fractures and both femurs were shattered and one arm broken. After resuscitation for a few days, he was very, very quiet. His local vicar had visited a number of times and he had told him the awful story about the deaths of his family. We were very worried because he appeared, however, to show no reaction at all. This went on for some 10 days. He was very co-operative but didn't say much at all so a psychiatrist was brought in to talk to him. Still he didn't talk. We did the best for him, as you would expect, trying to be as natural as possible, which was quite a task because he was virtually unable to do anything for himself.

The usual procedures had gone ahead, post-mortem and inquest, and one Tuesday afternoon the time came for them all to be buried in a plot together in the next village. After the service the Archdeacon of Wisbech came to talk to him to give him the details of the committal. Apparently he had a lot of friends and the whole town attended the service. He appeared, however, very calm afterwards and said little but thanked the Archdeacon. At 7.30 p.m., before I went off duty, I settled him down and said goodnight to him. Just as I was about to give the report, the senior matron phoned me to say the senior night nurse was off sick and she hadn't got a replacement. I protested but she could only leave me with a first-year pupil nurse on duty that night. The latter had come out of initial training just some two months previously and this was only her second night on duty. She was a quiet little thing of about 18 and had very little knowledge. I reminded the matron that today was the day that our patient's family had been buried and I couldn't foresee what would happen that night. She replied, 'Well you will have to stay on.'

So I stayed on until after midnight and made sure everything was all right. The road traffic accident patient seemed to be comfortable and quiet and appeared to settle down. We had two priests; both were vicars and were on the ward as patients at the time. One was moderately ambulant so I asked him very kindly to keep an eye on things in the event of trouble, and he agreed to do so with alacrity. So at 12 midnight I went off duty after having given the new lass as comprehensive instructions as I could.

Her duties in the morning were to take the tea round, take the patients temperatures and make sure the beds of the ambulant patients were made – not particularly onerous tasks and she should have been able to cope with this reasonably well. I went off duty, however, with a degree of apprehension and came back early the next morning at half-past six to find the ward in total chaos. The girl was sitting in the office pale and shaking. I looked straight into the ward but my accident patient was fast asleep.

'What happened?' I asked her.

She told me that he had woken up at 1.00 a.m., called her and wanted to hold her hand. She said he started talking about his family. He kept hold of her hand and wouldn't let go and didn't go to sleep until 5.30. 'Oh you poor girl!' I thought, 'Now you go off straight away and go to bed.'

She looked shattered. We'd been very clever, done all the smart things but it took an innocent, reasonably uneducated in nursing terms, a simple girl, to break down the barrier by just listening to him and holding his hand. Why hadn't we done that? Well, we heard him but I don't think we listened. Particularly we didn't listen to his silences. It was a salutary lesson to me. I think this was a major step in my development, which essentially made me decide to leave the profession to get closer to the patients by other means – but more of that later.

After this, the patient improved. He healed well and the last I heard of him was that he had left the country with his only surviving son and emigrated to Australia to a new life. But that poor lass – she left; she could take no more. It was so unfair of the system to place her in that situation, but the nursing profession had long been under-staffed and always threw people in at the deep end. Opportunities are missed because of the paucity of funds provided for the care of the sick in this country.

The vicar in the next bed to that patient was causing us some problems. He was all of sixteen stone, six foot tall and decidedly scruffy. Even when the Bishop came to visit him, he couldn't be bothered to shave. He was a nice, cheerful idiot but co-operative; he had a fracture of the head of his femur after long-term ingestion of a steroid for his supposed asthma. He had been prescribed the drug five years previously and someone had forgotten to take him off it so one day his leg just collapsed as he was coming out of the church. We received this lump of humanity to care for and each day, as we put him in the bath, it took about six members of staff to lift him. Each time we vowed we wouldn't do it again but really had no option. It was the recognised thing in those days that everybody had a bed bath or big bath daily.

One afternoon I was in the office with a colleague. It was quiet on the ward when there was a knock on the door. A rep. came in and introduced himself; he worked for a company which made patient hoists. In 1969 these were new to us and I had never seen one. The type he was selling is nowadays very well known as an ambi-lift, and it had a stretcher device included in the fittings which allowed just one person to lower a heavy, paralysed patient into the bath. I was most interested in this and asked if we could have a demonstration. The chap then offered to leave one with me for a month. The price of the equipment and all the fittings was £287, which, considering it was 1969, was a lot of money but not extortionate. We used it for some four or five days with great success on other patients as well as the vicar and it made life so much easier when it came to dealing with some of our immobile people.

The next day was the CO's inspection. He came into the ward with his entourage and the adjutant and saw the ambi-lift.

'What's that?' he asked.

I told him and showed it off to him.

'Get it out!' he said.

'What?' I said.

'Get it out! It's not official equipment so you are not insured and if anything happens, if anybody is injured, we will have a huge bill for compensation.'

So it had to go, much to our disappointment. Next day my colleague was putting the heavy vicar in the bath again when he hurt his own back so badly that he had to be admitted and was still flat on his back a month later. At the end of the month I went to collect the payslips from accounts and handed him his as he lay in bed. As usual he moaned about his deductions.

'Look at that!' he said, '£50 tax!'

The sum he was getting after deductions was remarkable enough – £287 for a month's salary.

'Can I have that?' I said. 'I want to take it to the adjutant.'

The adjutant listened to me as I pointed out that my colleague's pay amounted to the same as the cost of the lift.

'Okay, you've made your case but don't use unauthorised equipment again.'

Another lesson learned. But we got our ambi-lift and good value it was!

We had two very pleasant consultants in the Orthopaedic Department at the time. One was an American Lieutenant Colonel who was seconded to the RAF as an exchange officer and the other one, Group Captain Keir, was a Scot who was well liked by all. He had a persistent problem with his own orthopaedic condition, which caused him to limp badly, and he was always in pain. His attitude towards the patients was always kind and paternalistic and the patients thought the world of him. He was also a good surgeon and had good results in his surgery, but he did like peace and quiet.

One afternoon I was sitting in the office in the ward, which was full of young men who were mainly not ill but bored and as usual were making one dickens of a noise. You can always tell an orthopaedic ward by the noise that comes out of it. He came out of his office and said to me,

What's all that racket?'

'That's the patients, Sir.' I replied. 'They are enjoying themselves.'

'Oh!' he said and sat down, 'I suppose it's better than being miserable.'

I made him a cup of tea and we sat talking for a little while. He was tired; we had had some late nights operating and his leg was hurting. He looked through the window in the ward and said, 'I don't know if we do any good for these chaps.'

It was almost a classic case of despair at seeing the same old injuries again and again. However I replied that yes, it did help and the patients thought the world of him, didn't he know that? He looked surprised,

'Do they really?' he said.

'Yes,' I answered, 'You do something for them that most consultants would never do.'

'What's that?' he asked.

'Well,' I continued 'When you examine them, you sit on the bed with them and show them the problem on the x-ray. And then you stand up and you tap them on the shoulder and say, 'Okay boy, see you in the theatre tomorrow and we'll see what we can do for you.'

He looked at me puzzled and asked, 'Do I really?'

'Yes, that's what makes the difference. You touch them,' I told him.

He thought for a while and told me of his experiences in Edinburgh Royal Infirmary before the War. He worked for a consultant who was a very sincere Christian and each night this man would visit his patients on the next day's operating list and kneel down by their beds and pray that God would guide his hands while he operated on them. He said they were a really rough lot, a lot of working men in those days straight out of the poorer parts of Edinburgh. You would have thought they would have been petrified. He said he was a much loved man and the patients trusted him implicitly.

The American Colonel was a different kind of chap altogether. He got on well with us all and with the group captain too. He was a brilliant innovator, who brought a breath of fresh air into the Department. He was also more informal in his approach but didn't suffer fools gladly. You could discuss a lot of things with him and he tried to encourage my colleague and me to join the United States Air Force as nursing officers, but it proved to be too difficult to leave the Royal Air Force and emigrate to the USA. Added to that, in retrospect it probably would have only been out of the frying pan into the fire and we would have ended up in Vietnam. He was a good surgeon, the patients and staff liked him, and we were very sorry to see him go after his six months' stay with us. He also gave great parties, which were enjoyed by everybody – very democratic, from ward cleaners to the CO.

I had settled well into orthopaedics and was learning a lot but we also had a couple of beds which we used for dental patients and orthodontic work. Having spent some time in the plastic surgery department at Halton in 1964, I had gained some experience in this, but the majority of this type of work was still done at Halton or Nocton Hall near Lincoln. One day two patients were transferred to us from Nocton because the consultant there had gone on compassionate leave and there was no-one at Nocton to look after them. Both of these young men had fractured jaws. One had fainted on parade and fallen on the point of his jaw and the other one was a victim of a road traffic accident. They both arrived three days after injury. One had lost a lot of blood and needed a transfusion; the other was in a poor condition because his wounds had become infected. Both, of course, were unable to eat or drink properly. This was the problem.

In those days the fractures were usually splinted externally, using a series of rods and wires, and the upper and lower teeth had to be kept wired together. Two molar teeth were removed from the right jaw to allow for some food and drink to go through into the mouth. Naturally the face was swollen and the patient was distressed. A pair of wire cutters was always available by the bed to cut the splints in case of vomiting, and a very close watch needed to be kept on the patients. They had to be weighed daily and helped to clean their mouths, which became foul as a result of their inability to use their swollen tongues because of the pain. It was also difficult for them to talk and the usual treatment was to keep them slightly sedated so that they slept a lot, but still they needed constant observation. This presented us with a challenge and I tried to find an answer to their nutrition and hygiene, coming to the conclusion that if they were not hungry, they wouldn't have so much pain and they needed the nourishment to cope with their injury and help heal it.

At the time the first spacecraft was going into orbit and one evening on television I saw the crew eating from tubes of food with a straw. I realised that this method could be adapted and modified and we could feed these patients a good puree diet with plenty of fluid instead of using the usual method, which was to give them chicken soup with a spoon. They soon got fed up with this. The spoon hurt their mouths and banged on the splints and eventually they gave up eating. So I obtained a plastic nozzle some three inches long and a plastic food bag. I filled the plastic food bag with the pureed food, whatever was available, put the bag in hot water, fitted the nozzle on top of the bag and put the nozzle between the gap in their teeth. The patient could then squeeze and the food would slip through onto the top of their tongue so that they could swallow it easily. After completion of the meal, which they chose and which I let them liquidise themselves, the bag was then filled with a weak solution of bicarbonate of soda. The same thing happened; they squirted it into their mouth with the throat closed and dribbled it out through the same gap between the teeth, thereby cleaning the mouth of all the food debris. This method worked like a charm and the patients began to make good progress. The fractures and wounds healed rapidly and they started to put on weight. Added to this was the great psychological boost given to them by letting them take part in their own treatment, as well as allowing them to choose their own diet and use a liquidiser.

When the consultant came back from leave he was most impressed with the progress they had made and suggested that I write it up. I did this and presented it to the Air Ministry, which gave me an award of £40 from the RAF Innovations and Ideas Scheme. Quite a tidy sum in 1971. This information was then circulated as a paper around other RAF hospitals and also given to the National Health Service. What they did with it I don't know.

I was by now well into orthopaedics and beginning to find a lot of pleasure in nursing patients in plaster and traction. Also in the care of the bored, fit, young men; by and large the only time they were ill was when they were given an anaesthetic to correct their particular surgical problems. The rest of the time they needed something to take their minds off their immobile status, whatever the problem was. But it was still essential to keep a close watch on them even though they had no obvious worries.

One young man who had fractured his femur in a road traffic

accident, and had had his fracture plated by our American Colonel, began to behave in an untypical manner. He was about four days post-op. and became suddenly remote in his behaviour; he was surly and uncooperative and I felt that something was wrong. After I'd expressed my concerns to the Junior Medical Officer in charge, he went to look at him and examine him. He could find nothing wrong at all and he reassured me that all was well. I had a feeling that the young man was unwell and that something was wrong, as his behaviour did not improve. I took his temperature and blood pressure every hour to see whether there was anything there. This meant that someone had to attend to him hourly instead of the usual visits to the convalescent patient, which were only before mealtimes. At the end of the 24 hours we still had no definite answer to the problem. The blood pressure remained stable, the temperature didn't rise but, knowing the patient reasonably well, I was still unhappy. I voiced my fears to the Colonel the next morning when he did his rounds, so after he'd finished, he went to examine him fully. He came back to the office in a hurry and said,

'He's got a fat embolus!'

I had never heard of that in 1968 and a lot of people hadn't. He went on,

'Let's get his chest x-ray and see if there is any damage.'

When I asked him how he had known and picked it up so quickly, he showed me numerous little tiny petechial haemorrhages on the patient's skin folds round the arms and shoulders – small amounts of bleeding into the skin due to the body trying to deal with the problem by producing quantities of anti-clotting factor in the blood. The treatment was to give him a regulated dose of an anti-clotting factor, which brings the bleeding under control and allows the embolus to absorb on its own. This is, of course, not an unknown complication in large bone injuries when some fatty marrow from the bone gets into the bloodstream and blocks part of the circulation to the lung. The treatment worked and within a week the patient was responding well. It was a case of 'never ignore your sixth sense'. It was invaluable when caring for sick people. Really it's known as experience.

We were still living in Soham in the old vicarage and although I was enjoying the work at the hospital, I was beginning to get restless and wanted to work on my own and to make my own decisions. I reckoned that I always enjoyed teaching and instructing junior nurses and felt that it would be a good career development if at this stage I was to do a teaching course and become a registered clinical teacher. I was beginning to find that as my life changed every two years, it was becoming onerous to re-establish oneself each time I was posted – time consuming, hard work and demoralising until I could prove that I was quite capable of filling a new post confidently. When I spoke to the senior tutor about this, he advised me to have a word with the principal tutor of the RAF Nursing Branch, whom I had met before and with whom I had established a reasonable rapport. She turned out to be enthusiastic about my application and pointed out that if I did not do this, then I would be doing the same old thing on the wards up to the age of 55 and on leaving the Service, would stand little chance of gaining employment in a reasonable post in the National Health Service. Not strictly true, but there was an element of truth in it.

At the same time I considered leaving the Service and applying for work with one of the big drug companies, who were recruiting SRNs into their sales force. This application however turned out to be a blind alley, something of a rat race and the type of work that I found I could not subscribe to. The idea of selling drugs that didn't work to doctors who didn't want to know me or see me either was unappealing. So I applied for training and one Monday morning went to Ipswich to the Civic College for interview for acceptance onto a teaching course then available for clinical teachers. This was a semi-academic course with a high practical component, teaching on the wards and not in the classroom situation. It was designed to look for teaching opportunities, as they were called, in the daily work of the students in the ward. I had to submit a paper and then have a difficult interview. It struck me that even if the interviewers were not exactly antimilitary, they had little or no concept of the role of the Armed Forces. They were only aware of atom bombs and armaments and couldn't accept the idea of the defence of the realm. I thought they were all a bit left wing and my heart sank. However I hit back and was accepted for the course to start in September 1971. Actually the interviewers were cleverer than I thought at the time, and they were just goading me to see what I would say.

The acceptance came with the usual list of conditions, all the usual reading lists required and the pre-course preparation. Also I had to move away from the orthopaedic onto a medical ward in order to gain experience in the main medical conditions associated with pathology and in disorders to be found in the systems and functions of the body in sickness. It looked quite demanding and I wondered what I had let myself in for. Not having done any planned studying in nursing or medicine for some years, I did wonder if I had the staying power and the resources to cope with a year of intense full-time studying again away from home. The RAF approved my application and I was granted a year's study leave. I was to be accommodated during the week in the sergeants mess at RAF Wattisham near Ipswich.

It was now May and in my new post in the medical ward I began to find another area of study which was most interesting and gave me a great deal of pleasure. At about this time my wife's elderly aunt had died and had left her a small amount of money. My wife wanted a home instead of living in second-rate rented accommodation so we began house hunting. The bank manager who had advised us some time previously not to go into house purchase had been forced to eat his words because now house prices were beginning to soar and every day showed a market rise. Gazumping was becoming common. We had nearly missed the boat. However, in Ely itself, a new estate was being built. We looked at the properties and decided that we could afford a 4-bedroom home with all mod. cons. At the time we thought these houses were luxuriously equipped with fitted kitchens and bathrooms and that you only needed furniture. As we look back now, they were pretty spartan but to us they represented sheer luxury and all for just £5,650 – this price was quite ridiculous. It was easier to get a mortgage in 1971, so we moved into our new home in July and saw the price treble within a year; we had only just made it. However, although mortgage and insurance payments were only £45 per month, still that was quite a lot out of a salary of £150 a month. Anyway, we were happy with the house and were the envy of a lot of our friends. But they drank and smoked and we had learnt to be careful, so we coped. I was paying less for petrol now that we were actually living in Ely near the hospital. The boys remained at their school and went there on the bus, so they were happy. A new home and a bus ride daily – what more could they want?

I was happy on the Medical Ward. Many of our patients were civilians and, amongst other things, I had to learn the art of emergency resuscitation. Attached to the ward was a very high tech. intensive care unit which had to be staffed from the ward itself and was often in use. It had, for the time, rather a lot of high tech. electrical gadgets such as continuous recording ECG, blood pressures, blood gases and so on and so forth. These were all the products of the RAF's own Research Department. The RAF had an advantage over the National Health Service in having a major research centre dealing with aviation medicine, and the spin-off to general medicine was quite considerable. One also had a lot to learn with all this equipment. Certainly we had to trust the equipment but at the same time must not forget to observe the patient for other signs – a real trap for the unwary. I recalled the Air Commodore saying that when he went to a United States hospital in Boston and watched routine surgery with the patients all connected up to electronics, nobody had noticed that the patient was going blue until he pointed it out! I gained an insight into the care of patients and the treatment of diseases which would have been routine before, but now that they were carefully monitored with all this modern equipment and modern laboratory techniques, I was able to see slight critical changes in the patients' condition which, if not treated immediately, could lead eventually to long-term serious damage. This of course was the early 1970's. Much of this work was quite exciting and very scientific and I was in the middle of it.

Gradually I settled down and looked forward to the teachers' course, when I would be able to explore in some detail and in some depth the many concepts I was now picking up. However I had to spend the day before I was to start at Ipswich getting ready for my move to Wattisham, where I was due to arrive after my first day on the course. I also spent some time on that day looking at a Jaguar car of a friend of mine.

Ginger was a corporal trained nurse who worked with me on the ward and over the previous six months he had been found to have a chronic gut disease. He had been given steroids in quite heavy doses, which had helped, but each time they tried to reduce the dose, the disease flared up again so he remained on this heavy dose. One day he told me that he had decided to get a Jaguar car. He had a very nice little Triumph Herald in excellent condition but he wanted a Jag and he had found one in London, owned, he claimed, by a Jaguar engineer. I laughed at that and the fact that it was a London car, but he was convinced it was genuine. So one day he sold his Triumph and went and got the Jag.

'Well, where is it?' I asked.

'Oh,' he said, 'It's not the right colour for me so I'm having it re-sprayed in British racing green.'

He asked me to go and have a look at it that lunchtime but when we got to the garage it was closed. I could only get a glimpse of the car through the dirty window of the paint shop – it looked all right. Anyway, he eventually collected it but on the following Monday morning he came to work in a very bad mood.

'The wife won't go in it!' he moaned. 'She said if she was going to go in that she would want a fur coat and where was the Triumph anyway?'

He hadn't told her what he was doing. Now, of course, he was paying the price. I thought for a moment and then I said,

'Well if it's as good as you say it is, I will swap you for my A60. But I will need to spend a little bit of time on it to look it over.

ELY HOSPITAL

You bring it down to me and leave it with me on Sunday afternoon. You can take my car back on the Sunday but I must have it back by evening.' I was off early to Ipswich on the Monday morning.

On Sunday afternoon he arrived and the first thing I noticed was that it was not even taxed. He told me not to worry about that, it would be okay for a day. But I refused point blank to drive a strange, powerful car without any insurance or tax so I took him back to his quarter in my car and then came back home and looked it over. It was appalling: a lovely paint job but a corroded battery, holes in the door, underneath the sills filled in with fibreglass, two bald tyres, one plug whose actual setting was in a worn hole in the aluminium cylinder head with all the threads stripped off it. I did eventually get it started and just went up the road on our private estate and back again. The back axle sounded like a tank. I just couldn't believe it. I put it in my garage for safekeeping with a note to be given to Ginger when he collected the car, telling him what I had found. I was certainly not going to buy that. It was a puzzle to me why a rational, very law-abiding and sensible chap had done what he did and upset his wife so badly. However later on in the year, when talking it over with a pathologist, I was told that this change in behaviour was one of the known side effects of large regular doses of steroids. There were not only the physical results but quite often mental and personality changes. These were definitely not unknown and this was par for the course. At least it gave me a better understanding of steroids. I often thought of this when later on I saw people change personality after steroid therapy and was able to reassure worried relatives about what the drug was doing and how the patient would usually return to normality when they came off such potent drugs.

So having done this and having written the note, I went to bed at about 10 p.m. But life is never as simple as that and, as I was just going to bed, little did I know that within 24 hours I would be in the air evacuation team going to Cyprus, where I would be involved for some weeks so that I would miss my course.

As I went to bed, I watched the news on the television in the bedroom . . . it was depressing as usual. Four airliners had been hijacked in the desert by Arab terrorists. The Jordanian army was on the move south and the whole lot looked as if it was going to be a shooting match. I turned the news off and was just settling down to sleep when there was a knocking at the front door. I went down to find the orderly officer telling me to report to the hospital adjutant at once. He didn't know the reason for this, of course, so he said! Very reluctantly I arrived at the hospital to find everybody rushing around like scalded cats. An aeromed was being activated to go to Cyprus the next morning to collect the hostages from the hijackers. I protested that I was cleared from the hospital and was on my way to Ipswich in six hours but I was told that I was the only SRN in that hospital whose jabs were up to date and I would have to go. This was not true – one other SRN had refused to go, so I had to. I rushed home, parked my car outside my garage and broke the news to my wife, which naturally didn't go down well. I collected my kit and was picked up by staff car at about 5 a.m. and by 7 p.m. was at Lyneham. I was met by the SNCO in charge and introduced to the team of some 24 nursing attendants and one other SRN. All our documents were checked out and it was most annoying to find that I was indeed the only one of the 24 people to have my jabs up to date; none of the others had. Off we went to station sick quarters where the SMO was far too busy and said: 'Well, you'll have to give them. So I ended up doing all the jabs and getting everybody up to date. We then went to the other side of the airfield and spent the rest of the day loading three ambulances and all the mobile hospital equipment into a Hercules for take-off at 7 p.m. that night. We were all in civilian clothes (which were now a bit of a mess) and exhausted, but after a meal we were airborne at 2000 hours.

I had been so busy with all that had to be done that I hadn't noticed much else and by the time we sat in the webbing seats inside the Herc, I was beginning to feel very unwell. We had had to have a cholera boost, which I had given myself; my arm was

Aeromed evacuation unit, Cyprus, 1971. Author last on the right.

swollen and I was suffering and I had a temperature of 102 degrees Fahrenheit. There was nothing I could do but sweat. I remember going down to the tail section of the aircraft to have a pee and trying to avoid walking on the tail floor where it said in large notices in yellow 'Do not walk on these points.' To pee in a funnel sticking out of the skin of the aircraft, which was bounding around, was not only quite a feat but decidedly hairy and I was ill. I had visions of myself falling out of the bottom of the aircraft into 20,000 feet of space. However, after a most uncomfortable journey of some six hours, we arrived in Akrotiri in Cyprus and went straight to the station sick quarters and went to bed.

I was just drifting off to sleep when the movements officer came in and woke me up. I looked at him in rather a bleary way and he said,

'Have you got your car keys with you?'

'Oh dear, yes!' I answered.

'Well,' he continued, 'Your wife can't get your car out and open the garage.' Ginger's Jaguar was also in the garage and the poor chap had come down to get it. I handed the keys over and they were flown back by the next aircraft that went home.

We messed around in Cyprus for six weeks on one-hour standby. First the hostages were coming out, then they were not. The aircraft in which we were flying into Lebanon was the wrong colour for the Arabs and they wanted the RAF roundels removed and red crosses painted on instead. When that was done, they wanted them wiped out and replaced with a red crescent. All very frustrating but eventually a civilian aircraft was chartered and we were to go next day to Nicosia airport to travel in a big Canadair four-engine transport plane The night before we went, the SMO told myself and the other NCO that we could take only 12 personnel, as this was all the clearance we had got from the Lebanese. So we had to get 12 volunteers, preferring the single men. Moreover we knew that the two coloured chaps, who were both Hindu, would be totally unacceptable to the Arabs. It was obvious that then, as now, the multi-racial society law applied only to the UK. Nobody else bothers but it would have given us a problem then. I got them all on parade and told them there was a lot of shooting going on and it was highly dangerous, so no married chaps and unfortunately no coloured chaps. I then gave them the order to come to attention and volunteers to take one pace forward. Of course they all took one pace forward – so much for British youth! Well, I observed, I will have to select them myself using the existing criteria. The next day we went up to Nicosia where we were all kitted out in our flak jackets and we waited for the aircraft to land. As it landed it came over to the far side of the airfield, where we were to be picked up well away from any publicity. But unfortunately it collided with a runway light on a pole and smashed its starboard wing about 12 inches from the end . . . so that was the end of that. We returned to Akrotiri and found, to our surprise, that Middle East Airlines had flown out all the hostages anyway 12 hours earlier. So we sat down for another three weeks until the RAF movements people evacuated

Author practicing with the U.N. at Nicosia.

us back to the UK. The last three weeks of the attachment were quite pleasant; it was somewhat of a holiday visiting all the major tourist spots on the island.

When we arrived home six hours after we left Akrotiri, I went back to Ely. Obviously I had missed my course. There had apparently been an uproar about this, which had happened because a colleague of mine who was jabbed up to date had refused point blank to go and so had gone sick. There was talk of a Court Martial but it never came to anything. Still, he was not popular because everybody had to do their turn anyway. I returned to work on the ward and the course was postponed until the next year. It was no good starting then; the course was so intensive, I would not have fitted in at all after six weeks. Permission came through for study leave again about a week later, so I had another year to prepare.

In the meantime my wife had applied for a post at the local

hospital and had been accepted as a staff nurse. Our youngest was now 12 years old and we were therefore able to cope with this quite well now that the children were all at a reasonably responsible age. She fitted in very well at the Tower Hospital at Ely, having had previous experience at St. John's Hospital at Hillingdon in our Uxbridge days, and felt quite at home. So now we had to juggle our off-duty to get our home life properly organised.

I had only been back about two weeks when I was put on night duty for two weeks. This was a bit of a struggle now that my wife was also working, but we coped and, as it was getting towards Christmas, we invited my wife's elderly relatives for the holiday, which was only some six weeks away. But a month before Christmas I was told that I was the bar relief caterer in the mess over the Christmas period. This meant long hours at night and normal work during the day. I was most displeased. I had lost my course because of somebody else who refused to go on attachment and had got away with it. I had already done two weeks' night duty so I went to see the warrant officer to complain. He said:

'Tough, you're next so you go on!' I refused. He told me, 'Well, you know what will happen to you then, lad.' When I said the other chap got away with it, he replied, 'We're not talking about the other chap, we're talking about you.' He was just not interested. This was getting very upsetting and now we had to cancel our elderly relatives' visit if I was on duty over Christmas.

I didn't want to stand in the bar for seven nights selling beer. I returned to the ward and one of the MOs saw me and said I was looking fed up, what was the trouble? I told him and he said,

'Don't worry, I will give you a 624 medical report and put you on light duties until January.'

'Are you going to take the can for that?' I asked him.

I had already done him a favour by finding him a short let for his wife so that she could spend Christmas with him, so he felt he owed me a favour. The form went in and he saw me days later and said the adjutant and the warrant officer had got my documents out and were gunning for me but he said,

ELY HOSPITAL

'Don't worry! I will see you're okay. If I say you're sick, you're sick and there's nothing they can do about it.'

The warrant officer phoned me a week before the duty and reminded me that I would be on duty the following week, so I said that I wouldn't be there. He told me not to be stupid and to obey orders. It was getting nasty. The following evening the hospital registrar came to the ward to collect the documents for the next day's discharges. I went through them step by step with him. He was a wing commander, next in line to the CO. After we had done this, he said,

'Now about you. You've had light duties for a time and now you need a medical board because you will have to be downgraded if this persists and you'll not be eligible for promotion or to go on your course.'

I told him I would not be at the medical board because there was nothing wrong with me and he asked me why I had got a 624, then. He listened to my explanation, then asked a few questions and said,

'Okay, that's reasonable. They've treated you badly, in a very cavalier fashion. You won't do your duty over Christmas but you will have to do it in January.'

'I don't mind that,' I replied. And that was the end of that.

However the next chap in line for duty was the one who had refused to go on attachment, so he had to do it. The biter was truly bit! He threatened me with everything but death but he had no option, so he did the duty and I did it in January.

I was working very hard now, doing a lot of study and research for the course. The ward work, as I gained knowledge, was getting more interesting but I was also beginning to feel in myself that while a lot of what we did did not fail, it did not quite succeed either. People felt better but the progress of the disease continued. As strange as it may seem, it struck me that everybody was getting older and we were trying to stop the ageing process but we couldn't – it was inevitable. As the medical profession looked upon a patient's death, by and large, as a failure, I was now beginning to think that as everybody we looked after had to die in time, surely a good death was not a failure but a success, and the quality of life was what really mattered. It was no good fighting death if the life we extended had no quality to it and our role therefore, in the end, was to give comfort and support even if the treatment didn't work. One evening a little old man some 65 years old called Fred was admitted to the ward suffering from a sub-arachnoid haemorrhage near the brain. This is a painful and distressing problem, usually brought about by the wear and tear of the arteries of the covering of the brain. He was very restless, in great pain and only semi-conscious. So it was decided by the consultant, after all the necessary injections, tests and so on, to sedate him and let his body rest. An intravenous drip of a sedative agent was commenced. A full nursing care schedule was started and after three days he was quiet. He was asleep 24 hours a day and one evening, as his condition did not appear to be improving, his wife, rather a large woman, came into the office and asked me if I could get a form filled in. She handed me the form,

'What's it for?' I enquired.

'It's his life insurance,' she said rather grudgingly.

'But he's not dead,' I said.

'He will be soon,' she snapped. Naturally I refused point blank to take it off her and she stormed out. 'I'm going to get my daughter to see you,' she threatened, 'She works at Addenbrooks.'

Next evening a timid young woman about 24 years old came into the office and announced herself. She was the old man's daughter and, indeed, she did have an Addenbrooks scarf on, but what she did there I'd no idea. She could have been a cleaner for all I knew. I offered a seat, which she declined, and then she said,

'Are you hiding something from us?'

I looked at her in disbelief.

'Don't you think that a sub-arachnoid haemorrhage is enough?' I enquired gently. She went red, turned on her heel and left the office.

Another couple of days went by and the sedatives were stopped. One morning the patient, Fred, woke up as bright as paint, said he felt really well, just a bit stiff in his joints. His wife and daughter didn't want to know and had stopped visiting him. In a week he was up and about and wandering around the ward – he had improved so quickly. He needed a bit of help with the physiotherapist but after a fortnight he was ready for discharge. He would need a bit of help at home, so the social worker collected him one morning and took him off with his bits and pieces to see what his home was like and to see if he would be all right. Half an hour later she was back. The wife had refused even to allow him over her threshold. The home was a council house, absolutely immaculate apparently, with wall to wall carpets, something quite strange in 1972 for a working man's home. He didn't live there, declared the wife, and showed the social worker where he lived, in a shed at the bottom of the garden. It was a nice shed apparently, but totally unsuitable for our chronic invalid. So we couldn't discharge him. The social worker then went to find out whose name was on the rent book of the house and she discovered that the house was in Fred's name. That meant that he had a legal entitlement to enter his own home. When the wife was interviewed again by the social worker, she told her that the next day she would be bringing Fred home and bringing a policeman with her and she would have to let him in.

'Over my dead body,' retorted his wife. 'I have scrimped and saved to make this a comfortable home and he has dirty habits.' The next day Fred was discharged and this time, when they arrived at the house accompanied by a member of the local constabulary, she'd gone and was never seen again. Fred moved in and had a high old time bringing in his friends and having a lot of parties until, about one and a half years later, he was found dead in bed. However, he'd had the best eighteen months of his life. Truth is indeed stranger than fiction.

There were indeed some strange people in the Fens but then there's nowt as queer as folks in any part of the country. Mr Evans, aged about fifty-five, was a well-to-do farmer from Lincolnshire who was absolutely bright yellow with liver failure and desperately ill. His main diet was whisky and his liver was

R.A.F. Hospital, Ely in 1976.

now like a bit of leather. After some two months' treatment, most of his jaundice had gone and he was beginning to improve but getting a bit restless. He was permanently constipated and required all kinds of unmentionable treatments to get his gut working, much to his discomfort. He told the Air Officer Commander in Chief on his annual visit that the only thing he didn't like in the ward was my index finger. The mystified AOC asked me what he meant and as I explained, the AOC went a little green. On the main Tuesday round Mr Evans told the consultant Group Captain that he had to be out by Saturday. He was told he was not fit enough and wouldn't be well enough for some time yet but he persisted and the Group Captain asked him why the urgency,

'I'm going to a wedding on Saturday,' he said in his broadest Lincolnshire accent, 'and I'm going to sit on my wife's grave outside the church when they come out.'

'When who comes out?' enquired the Group Captain.

'My son,' he said. 'While I've been in here, he's been knocking off my fiancée and he's got her pregnant and he's going to marry her. I'm going to be sitting on the grave of my wife by the church door when they come out. That will learn him.'

Needless to say he didn't do this as he was far too unwell and it was some six months before he was transferred to Kings College Hospital in London for further treatment in their liver unit.

The rest of the year passed pleasantly enough. I did my usual stints of night duty and station duties and worked hard. Our new house was maturing well, my wife was enjoying her work at the hospital and my daughter was finding that school was not exactly enjoyable but was acceptable. My eldest boy was doing very well at the grammar school and was well thought of there. My middle son was coping. So all in all we were quite happy.

CHAPTER 9

Further Education

September arrived and, with another colleague who had applied for the course, I arrived at Ipswich City College to the world of academe and hopefully ready to put my foot on the ladder of promotion to higher things. I'd already applied for a commission and been turned down. There was a lot of competition and I was one of about ten who applied but the chap who got it eventually regretted it.

The Ipswich course was made up of all senior nurses, who came from a broad range of hospitals in the UK. In fact there were two nurses who came from Southern Ireland, both of them very gentle people and quite delightful, both nuns. Our tutor to the group was a Miss Roley, a grey-haired tall lady. She was one of the most balanced and perceptive people I've ever known and oh so polite. She told us we could call her Phyllis. As if we could! You didn't call people like her by their first name. We couldn't have called her that, it would have been embarrassing . . . She was always Miss Roley to us. Her sidekick was Brian. He could be called Brian! He was a nice chap who ran around after her and was most pleasant and amiable but hardly NCO material. He was clever, however, and had a more than adequate knowledge of his subject. Our main classroom was on the top floor of the eight-storey building. Here I came in contact with students in further education and what a funny lot I found them to be! We as nurses were much of a muchness, but to say that there was a rich diversity among the other six hundred or so students at the college would be an understatement. There were students of everything from sociology to engineering, cookery to child care and so on. But we had little time for socialising, being too busy, and the tasks we were set, although very interesting, were time-consuming. It was as well that we were not living at home but spent the week working, while the weekend was used for relaxing with the family.

The course proved to be a bit of an eye-opener. The subjects that we studied were, as much as anything, ourselves and our reactions to the student. It seemed to be a common fact that everybody who had applied for the course and had been accepted was articulate and had some experience of teaching. So a lot of self-knowledge was required as well as techniques in dealing with one's own fears. The students were taught, along with what was known as normal and disordered body function, educational psychology, teaching techniques and opportunities and other such related educational subjects. Reasons why people learn and did not learn were explored in depth and strategies worked out to cope with all the very many problems in education, which we often learned by role play. Visits to other hospitals and other departments, schools and colleges were undertaken and video, which was becoming accepted as a method of teaching at that time, was used. It was quite chastening to see ourselves as the others saw us.

However it was not all grind. Each week we had one afternoon devoted to what was known as liberal studies. We had a choice and I opted for English poetry. The tutor for this, a Mr Melling, was a very long-suffering chap who really opened my eyes to what had been to me anathema in school. I developed a love for English poetry which I'm sure will never leave me. Having been brought up in the Non-conformist Church, I had listened to thousands of sermons and knew something about what is good and what is bad in public speaking. I had learnt to string words together. Miss Roley said to me once that one of my discourses sounded very much like a homily, but then it's difficult to try and teach an old dog new tricks. I was, after all, some forty-two years of age and had had a lot of practice.

I realised somewhat late in life that I was capable of speaking to large groups without notes, relying on memory, but of course this was not good enough when teaching students to understand, rather than to learn just by rote, so that they could actually use the material that we gave to them. My main discovery was that an awful lot of this apparently new work was only confirming what I had already worked out for myself and this was now being put into a logical order for me. Miss Roley said to me one day that I was as if a cork had been taken out of the bottle and I was bubbling over. I thought for a moment and I said,

'What you mean is I talk too much,'

'You said it!' she laughed. 'But do give the others a chance and listen a little bit more carefully.'

I think the problem with life in the RAF, with its formal codes of practice, was that one never really had the opportunity to question. Now I could. I had few problems with most subjects apart from chemistry, which I loathed at school and many of the main principles of which I could not grasp. Apart from this, I learned enough to pass the exams. But it did give me a much broader and intelligent overview than I had had at school, where learning was mainly by rote.

We visited a number of other establishments, educational and otherwise, and I spent two two-week periods, one at the Hammersmith Hospital and the other at Bury St. Edmunds, under the eyes of a mentor who was a tutor. It was very interesting to see how other people worked in their hospitals, which I always compared to the RAF hospitals. They all seemed to be short of resources and their staff accommodation always seemed to me to be sub-standard.

One of the most interesting visits was to a famous hospice in London. We went down by coach and arrived early as a group. The Director of Studies – nothing so downmarket as a Senior Tutor here – was quite snooty and told us we were a half an hour early, so we should go for a walk and come back at 2 p.m. There was quite a number of other groups, including a church group who had a canon in charge of them, and a Salvation Army group, all associated with hospitals or hospices. My colleague and I walked around the area, which was in a quite well-off part of London, but I was disgusted with the amount of dogs' mess on the pavement and we spent some time navigating through this lot. Apparently other people did the same. When we got back to the hospice, we were actually allowed in and on this very hot humid afternoon sat in a big circle around the Director of Studies, who was quite obviously not enjoying the company of another lot of inquisitive idiots. After about a quarter of an hour of this it was getting warm and my mind was wandering. Suddenly my friend nudged me and whispered, 'What's that smell?' I sniffed, 'Oh dear, dogs mess!' We both looked sheepishly at our shoes – not us! The smell was getting stronger and suddenly my eyes lit on the culprit. The Canon had trodden in something and it was now wrapped around his boot. He noticed it at the same time as we did and he went pink, stood up, excused himself and hobbled out, to our intense amusement. I can remember little else about the talk. That overcame any learning situation possible and afterwards we all had a good laugh outside, including, I must admit, the Canon.

After visiting the ward, we saw what the staff were doing to cope with the terminally ill and I was much surprised to find that what we had been doing quite routinely in 1966 at Uxbridge, these people were doing now and they were taking a lot of credit for it as though they had invented it. I only wished we had written up some of that work at Uxbridge at the time, as a lot of terminally ill patients would have been helped by our knowledge in the ensuing years.

And so we came to exam time. The exams proved to be demanding but it is my contention that a hard exam is one in which you haven't done the work and don't know the answer and an easy one that in which you know it all. However, there were three days with three papers and a viva, and at the end I felt as if I'd done my best. I was recalled a fortnight later to take the viva again to get me into a higher grade, but I qualified and was able to add the distinction of RCNT after my name and felt very pleased with myself. It had been an eye-opening course. Not only had I learned a lot about myself, but also a lot about that strange creature, the student. I also had it confirmed in everything we did and talked about that we were forgetting people, concentrating on their diseases, and this had got to change. I learned that it was not the disease that mattered so much as the way the patient reacted to the disease. This was a major step again in my road to self-awareness. So I left Ipswich after a very fulfilling year, with a lasting affection for that dirty old town, and headed off into the unknown to await my new position in education.

CHAPTER 10

Teaching

After two days back at home in Ely my new posting came through. It was to the RAF hospital at Nocton Hall, near Lincoln. So I was off again, but this time to live in the mess as we had no intention of moving and upsetting the children and my wife and my wife's new career at the Tower Hospital at Ely. I arrived at the School of Nursing at Nocton to find Ted, with whom I had served in Gan, and Jack Noble, whom I'd heard of, both great fun, both well respected members of the staff. There was a lady civilian clerical officer in post so this small school was well served with staff.

The hospital was only training SENs and we had about three courses going through the year. So every two months we had a block of teaching for each course of about four weeks ... Certainly I had enough to do. Jack had really got it sorted out and it was a well organised Department, as it should be. He worked so hard and we were all happy and efficient. I remember when I joined, I was interviewed initially by the CO. He was a humourless wing commander who knew nothing about nurse education and told me what he expected of me. What he said was a load of rubbish so I said 'yes sir, no sir' and left. The senior matron was one of the Princess Mary's whom I had known years previously in the plastics centre at Halton, so she was quite familiar. It was a small family, the RAF Medical Branch then, and you couldn't move far without meeting somebody you had met at some time. I had to learn quickly. Jack went on leave as soon as I was posted in and Ted disappeared for hours at a time and left me holding the baby, but learn I did. The administration of nurse training under the auspices of the GNC, the civilian training body for nurses, was quite different to the

RAF administration but it was interesting to see how it was done.

I started well. My room in the mess was most comfortable and the mess itself was extremely friendly, with an excellent cook and, apart from being away from home except for weekends, life was quite pleasant. The work was no problem. I found that I had not only been well trained at Ipswich, but having had such a lot of experience under my belt, I could offer not only knowledge at the right level when teaching but also many anecdotes to illustrate the points I made. This was certainly better than the daily routine of the wards, of dealing with the stomach churning emergencies one encountered so many times, which left one exhausted. This was nursing by proxy. I told them what to do but had the expertise to back it up and when working on the wards and supervising the nurses, I could show the pupils that I could do all the things that I had taught them to do. My relationship with the senior staff was also much improved. I was now better qualified than most of them and I could now do things that they could not do and tell them what to do on training matters. Every word was listened to and usually acted upon. One had to be careful, to some extent, because of the differences in rank, but I had now been promoted to chief technician after a series of trade tests, which did not really stretch me very far.

Social life in the mess was good and I was able to get out and about with Ted a lot in the evenings and a number of times we went to Jack's home for the evening. For the first time in my life I got drunk. Jack was a great home wine-maker. He asked Ted and me round one evening to sample some of his apple wine, which was ready to drink. When we got there, he had to apologise. Four of his six bottles had exploded when he got them out but the two remaining were available and so we started on these. They were superb. I have never tasted anything so smooth. We then went on to his pea pod wine and the evening became very hazy. I remember going upstairs to the loo and being unable to feel my legs, and then floating down again. The next thing I remember is that I was back at the mess, where I woke up fully clothed the next morning with a hangover. Never again, I declared, but it was fun while it lasted. Jack and Ted were most amused, which didn't help, and I avoided Jack's tipples in future although they were always on offer.

The Hospital Warrant Officer was Dai Jones; he was the same one who had made a mess of my posting to El Adem some three years previously. He was a good bloke really and we had some fun together in the mess. He had a new Renault which he had bought at Doncaster some six months before and one day the engine exploded. He asked me if I could take him up to Doncaster one evening to pick it up when it was repaired. Ted went with me and we arrived at last after what had turned out to be a most horrendous journey through the thickest fog we had ever known. As we started back with Dai following us, the fog got so thick that we lost him and didn't arrive back until midnight. As we were having a drink in the mess before turning in, the phone rang – it was Dai. Just after we had left him the car had blown up again . . . Could we come and fetch him even though he didn't know where he was? What could we do but to go and look for him. It was early morning before we arrived back, but old Dai was now our friend for life. All good fun and all part of the day's work.

I was really beginning to enjoy life at Nocton. I stayed there for a year and then two people were posted out of RAF Hospital, Ely. The Group Officer Principal Tutor, as she now was, posted me back to Ely, which was just what I had been hoping for. The officer IC was an old friend of mine at Uxbridge; he was a flight sergeant then and we got on well, but he was only in post for a month when he was posted and replaced by another officer whom I knew by reputation but had never met before. This was a chap called Roy Vatcher, who was very progressive in his views. We looked forward to some interesting innovations in the training. He was also a very friendly man.

We were also training student nurses at Ely alongside a much smaller group of pupil nurses and I was expected to participate in their education also. This was the first time I had taught students in a classroom setting. There was a great emphasis on the academic studies but, interestingly, the previous staff had not really encouraged a lot of participation by the students in their own education and it was rather hard work to get them going. However, by a process of stealth, we gradually got them to start thinking about what they were doing and to encourage them in the art of lateral thinking. For example, to make an impact on the subject of cardiac-arrest resuscitation procedures, I suggested we made a film of a fictitious situation with all the usual participation of director, props, manager, lighting and so on. This was taken on board with great enthusiasm. We also started a monthly newssheet which highlighted news items with medical emphasis gleaned from newspapers, and attempted to amplify them and comment upon them for the benefit of our nursing and medical colleagues on the Service side. However, as often happens, while these were taken up with great enthusiasm, other areas began to suffer and we had to cool it all down a little. But we had learnt a

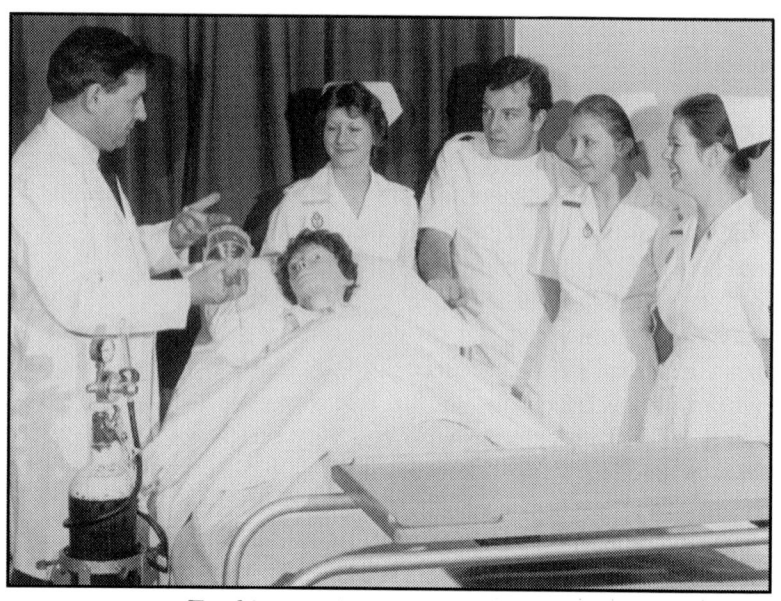

Teaching pupil nurses at Ely in 1977.

TEACHING

valuable lesson and were able to incorporate these ideas to great advantage in nurse education.

I spent some time trying to get the pupils interested in the concept of infection and its spread and control. I looked for a system that was more than just a concept but something which acted as a visual aid and made an immediate impact. I wanted to find something that acted as a marker for infection and could show the pupils exactly how infection spread away from the primary source and how easily it was carried on vectors and the distance it would also carry. Eventually I found that I could do this by the use of a simple substance which fluoresces under ultra-violet light and that substance was an ordinary household detergent powder. It was put in a bed between the two sheets and sprinkled over a model patient and his bedclothes. Two nurses then changed the bed. The powder, which is virtually invisible to the naked eye, could be traced by using an ultra-violet lamp. The grains of powder glowed with little points of light. This proved a great success and I was able to demonstrate how, on completion of just a simple thing like a bed change, the powder had spread not only to the nurses hands but up their noses, all over their uniform, shoes, into their hair and the surrounding bed space, sometimes up to a distance of 10 feet in all directions, as well. If they went to the next bed without washing their hands, it would spread onto that bed and its patient as well. It was quite an eye-opener to all of us to see how a simple dust spread and the risk of cross infection now became obvious.

This type of work was very interesting and took up a lot of time as we worked on some simple problems, often teaching subjects well documented in text books to those of lesser academic ability. Such pupils needed something practical to encourage them so that they could see the problem and digest the information. At the time a lot of controversy had been generated in the nursing press about pressure sores. Up to then, the skin of the pressure point on the patient's body was washed two or three times a day with soapy water and methylated spirits rubbed in to harden the skin. Talcum powder was then applied to dry it. But the new idea was that rubbing the skin caused a shearing effect which could actually make pressure sores worse and in fact cause them to happen, with subsequent ulceration, by damaging surface blood vessels. All kinds of ideas were being put forward to cope with this, the main one being that the immobile patient should be turned frequently in bed to give all the skin surfaces a chance to recover from the pressure which deprived the skin of its blood supply. I felt that we needed firstly to see where the pressure was occurring and, after a lot of experiment, developed a water-filled pad using an old intravenous drip bag attached to a simple manometer which was full of coloured water. We placed this under various parts of an immobile patient to see where the highest pressure was. This again proved to be quite a surprise to pupils and students alike, who thought that the only pressure areas were the buttocks, whereas we found that the shoulders and the back of the head had almost the same degree of risk as the buttocks. This, of course, was dismissed by the conservative element and the profession locally as a waste of time because they already knew this, but I maintained that it had never been quantified before and this, in fact, achieved exactly that result.

The profession was changing. We had far fewer nurses now in our intakes and the treatment of patients was changing too. Most patients were now out of bed as soon as possible after operation and discharged quickly, so a great number of the beds were occupied only by the very ill and the sick. The risk to a greater number of sick patients was becoming evident but it took a lot of effort to point this out to the authorities – more intense nursing care for the same number of patients and a decline in the number of nurses. I recall one instance when the Matron asked me what we were going to do if intake numbers reduced further. However, the intake per year was now being cut regularly. In the following spring we had in one month only fifty nurses on the wards to care for some 250 patients. The matron pointed out that this was the busiest time of year in the hospital as all the do-it-yourself enthusiasts, gardeners and golfers got outside and were admitted in droves with fractures and heart attacks and so on. I suggested

TEACHING

to her that we obtain the figure of the monthly admissions in the past two years from the Registrar's Department to give us an overview. The chief clerk's office was quite helpful, and with these figures I found that the admission numbers, plus or minus about 5%, did not vary over the months at all. There were fewer heart attacks in the winter but more bronchitis, more heart attacks in spring but fewer fractures caused by icy roads and so on. The matron was most unhappy when I showed her this and said 'How can I make a case for more staff when our submission is just the same each month?' I replied 'That's the best case you can make, a steady increase in the sickness of the same number of patients and a lowering of staff levels to do exactly the same work.' She made her case and we got another intake of nurses per year.

Another problem was to keep the pupils and students happy and aware of what important people they were. The honours and award system did not really cover this and I felt that we should have a decent prize-giving for finalists with an important personage to present the badges and certificates. This was taken up enthusiastically and we had some very nice times with the pupils and students' families attending, and photographs of each group with some very important people presenting the badges and awards.

The annual General Nursing Inspection was now upon us. We had numerous inspections over the years, Air Officer Commanding, Air Officer Commanding in Chief, Matron in Chief, Command Medical Officer and so on. But the General Nursing Council Inspection was the one that decided if we were to keep our nurse-training licence. Documentation had to be available for these inspectors – all training records, details of the way in which all the students were being treated. A complete breakdown of our curriculum had to be available to show that we were following the syllabus correctly. It involved a lot of time and effort. The RAF were justifiably proud of its nursing services and wanted to maintain its high standards. We did work hard to maintain this and we were highly thought of by the National Health Service patients in the area. These, given a choice, preferred to be admitted to Ely rather than Addenbrooks Hospital. I think this, however, apart from all other considerations, was because we were about a quarter of the size of a teaching hospital and therefore more friendly.

The inspections came and went and we did well, but after the inspection the Group Officer told me that she wanted me to go back to Nocton Hall for two months detachment because the tutor there had left and there was a new tutor recently qualified in post on his own. When I arrived I found a very bemused man, newly qualified, who was trying to do what he only half understood as he was new. But to my horror, Nocton's General Nursing Council Inspection was in two weeks. I hadn't been told that! That was a very busy fortnight but we pulled it all together and the inspection went like clockwork. After a lot of sorting out, I went back to Ely to find Roy talking about leaving and a new tutor, Ray Welton, being posted in. Roy subsequently left and went to Addenbrooks and Ray took over. He was a very gregarious chap, full of life and very enthusiastic and indeed great fun. He came from Liverpool and had a true Liverpudlian sense of humour and our days became full of laughter.

I was really settled in now. It was 1976. My boys were coming up to 'O' levels and my wife was now a ward sister and acting nursing officer at the Tower Hospital in Ely. The work was going well at the School of Nursing but, apart from rumbles of change on the horizon, the storm clouds were gathering for the nursing and medical profession in the Air Force. It looked as though the end of the medical services was not too far off. Most punters could only really see another ten years ahead; medicine was becoming more expensive and the number of personnel in the Service was dropping as new techniques came in. These relieved people from labour-intensive jobs and they became redundant. In July of that year I was put on the PWR for overseas again. There was only one hospital now overseas that was training nurses and that was at Wegberg in Germany. Unfortunately I didn't now want to go, with the family settled and our home functioning well, and educationally and workwise I was very happy.

TEACHING

A colleague of mine of the same rank and trade had been posted for a year's unaccompanied tour to Cyprus, looking after the troops from Troodos. This surprised me because we were screened only for educational purposes and he was an expensive, highly trained tutor going to do this kind of work. I phoned him up and he told me it had come out of the blue. I asked him if he would like to swap with me because I knew I was going to Wegberg. He was delighted and agreed, so I wrote to the Personal Management Centre requesting an exchange of postings. About two weeks later the adjutant called me to his office and said he had got the reply. It stated quite boldly that I was screened for three years. I already knew that and there were no vacancies for people in my trade to be posted unaccompanied out of the trade, so I was to forget it! As far as I was concerned, this was a blatant lie and I was most upset. The adjutant asked: 'What are you going to do then? Fill in one of these!' and he handed me a form for premature voluntary discharge to a pension at 22 years, which I was completing by the following year in June. I went home and discussed this with my wife and decided that enough was enough. I could easily get a job at one of the local teaching hospitals and my pension would make up the shortfall of salary on leaving the Air Force. This was one of the times when you realised that the system was bigger than the man. I was disappointed but didn't like being lied to. However I left it for a while to apply. I was going to apply in October unless I heard of any change. My posting to Wegberg was for the following February, so I had plenty of time.

The next excitement was being posted on a short detachment to the Navy, at the Royal Navy submarine base, to learn all about radiation safety. There was a requirement for x number of personnel in each unit to be 'competent persons', as it was known, to deal with nuclear war incidents in which medical problems arose. It proved to be a most interesting and instructive course. Life with the Navy is always pleasant; they're good company, as they should be; they are still the finest Navy in the world. A lot of that depends upon morale, which was high and always seems to be high. On return I was put in charge of all the radiation safety equipment in the hospital and the staff training schedule in the event of a nuclear incident. Again quite good fun, but quite a lot of work was needed to bring it up to date, with all the paperwork to do and my job in the school as well. The radiation set-up needed a complete overhaul in both personnel and equipment. We had a new CO, Group Captain Donald, who was a very pleasant and helpful man and I received a lot of support from him. The Radiation Safety Officer, however, was not quite so helpful and it took a lot of arm-twisting to get him going. As far as he was concerned, it was all a bore – he was a surgeon and that's all he wanted to do.

After the reorganization, which took me some three months, I asked the CO if we could have an exercise to check it all so as to see if it was working. He was most enthusiastic and we arranged the admission of a casualty (who was well primed) at 8.30 one evening. The only other person who knew about this was the matron and I got her on my side. So the balloon went up at 8.30 and all the duty staff were alerted. The Radiation Safety Officer was the last to appear, very annoyed and upset,

'What's going on?' he snarled at me.

'We are practising a radiation incident,' I answered.

'I'm supposed to be baby-sitting,' he said. 'I've had to walk out on the kids. Who organized it? You?'

'No,' came the CO's voice in the background, 'I did!'

'Oh,' said the Radiation Safety Officer, 'Yes, we do need a test,' he agreed, climbing down off his perch, and then he got to work. I knew exactly what was going to happen and I'd sketched out a full report before the incident and after the exercise I sat down and filled it all in. It was finished by midnight and I got our corporal clerk to complete it in typing in the morning. I took it to the Commanding Officer by 10 o'clock and he was most pleased. I earned a few brownie points on the way. I then told him that I thought that there would be a major exercise sometime. I had been warned by a friend I had made at the submarine base that we were going to be included in the next one for the group, and

TEACHING

he had given me the date and time. The CO asked me when I thought it would be and I said I thought it would be on such-and-such a date and at such-and-such time, but taking all things into consideration and all things being equal, if I heard any more I would let him know. And of course it happened bang on the dot! The system, which had been modified after the first exercise, worked very well and we were congratulated on our efficiency and of course the CO got the praise as it was his unit. More brownie points all round!

My posting was confirmed in late August so I put in my application for discharge, which was accepted. I was due to leave the Service on June 18th 1977 after completing 22 years. One day after this confirmation, I was in the Warrant Officer's office having a chat and happened to glance at the duty list that the clerk was typing. This was the Christmas duty list and I was down for mess treasurer for the month of December. 'Oh dear, they are going to get their money's worth out of me', I thought! Then I saw that the next person for January was the same chap who had fouled up my course by refusing to go on the detachment to Cyprus. I went back to the school and had a word with Ray, the boss, and asked if, as I was entitled to a month's resettlement course, I could go over Christmas as this would be most convenient for the school. I could go and spend the month at Addenbrooks and get used to the ideas of the National Health Service again. He thought that was very reasonable and would save an awful lot of bother at Christmas. It was a slack time and there were no students in, and it wouldn't get in the way. I applied through the usual channels, and to Addenbrooks, and was accepted. It went onto the personnel occurrence records at Ely and so became law. It was still on the station standing orders however that I was mess treasurer at Christmas and two weeks before December the Warrant Officer phoned me up and reminded me that I was mess treasurer. I said, 'I'm posted. I'm detached all of December. Its all in PORs.'

He checked and said oh yes you're quite right, oh well not to worry; the next chap will have to do it. I laughed to myself – it couldn't happen to a nicer chap, I thought. He of course was furious again and threatened me with everything but death just as he had done before. I smiled. That was that. It was a salutary lesson in not letting your mates down. So my course came and went. It was a bit of a waste of time but I was entitled to it. The four weeks passed quite quickly. I then applied to Peterborough District Hospital for a post advertised for a teacher of pupil nurses and was accepted. So I left the RAF on May 15th and again joined the National Health Service.

Postscript

It was a sad time indeed leaving the RAF. It had been my home for some 22 years and most, if not all, of what I had done I had enjoyed. It had been a struggle at times bringing up a family whilst on the move. Certainly, we had our difficulties, but it was all part of the journey to maturity. When I look back now over the years, I realise that I should be grateful for my upbringing, which instilled in me a sense of duty and respect for authority, not always for the person holding the position of authority, and my religious beliefs, which had guided me so often in difficult circumstances,. I was thankful also for my very detailed and worthwhile initial training in the National Health Service, which seemed to cover most situations and had given me the technical expertise to function well. I realise how lucky I have been to have had such a well balanced career and to have rubbed shoulders with a wonderful variety, mostly of very good people.

My own journey of learning to accept life as it is developed as I got older. The brash know-it-all at 21 years old, I hope, turned into a competent, thinking person. I was now able to view with hindsight my own actions in the early days with some embarrassment and shame at what I had done or said. But I had to acknowledge that, in the end, I had done my best for poor bleeding humanity and hopefully this will be recognised by readers of this saga. All this formed the base of my subsequent civilian career in nurse training from 1977 to 1992, until I was able, after an interminable course in traditional Chinese medicine, to leave the nursing profession. I then became an independent practitioner in my own right, able to make my own decisions and to treat patients accordingly.

All in all they were good years and I wouldn't change them for anything, even if I were to be given another chance.

I have now been in practice in acupuncture for sixteen years, but that's another story.